A Guide to Successful Workers' Compensation Case Management

A Guide to Successful Workers' Compensation Case Management

Dorothy Consonery-Fairnot

MSHA, BS, RN, CCM, CLNC

BOOKLOGIX®
Alpharetta, Georgia

Copyright © 2012 by Fairnot & Associates Healthcare Consulting, LLC.

All rights reserved. No part of this book may be reproduced or transmitted in any form or by any means, electronic or mechanical, including photocopying, recording, or any information storage and retrieval system, without permission in writing from the author.

ISBN: 978-1-61005-214-6

Library of Congress Control Number: 2012913011

Printed in the United States of America

∞This paper meets the requirements of ANSI/NISO Z39.48-1992 (Permanence of Paper)

This resource guide was developed to serve as a quick reference specifically for case managers who work in the field of workers' compensation. The state case management rules and regulations cited here were researched and selected topics were adapted from each state workers' compensation website. Topics and information included in this guide were specifically chosen with the intent to provide answers to the most frequently asked questions that affect everyday case manager activities. It is not intended to be used as a substitute for legal advice on specific case management practice. In the case of any inconsistencies, the statutory and regulatory state provisions should prevail.

This book is dedicated to the loving memory of my parents, Joseph and Celeste Consonery, whose wisdom has traveled with me throughout my life.

You talk when you cease to be at peace with your thoughts.

- Khalil Gibran

TABLE OF CONTENTS

Foreword xi

Preface xiii

Acknowledgments xv

Introduction.. xvii

Continuing Education Credits... xix

Chapter 1: Overview of Case Management..1

Chapter 2: Coordinated Team Approach to Workers' Compensation Case Management........5

Chapter 3: Workers' Compensation Case Manager Qualifications 15

Chapter 4: Organizations that Refer to Case Management Services 19

Chapter 5: The Initial Injured Workers' Interview Process...27

Chapter 6: Documenting Case Management Services 35

Chapter 1 – 6 Summary 51

Chapter 7: State-by-State Workers' Compensation Case Management Regulations ...55

State-by-State Regulations Table of Contents 61

Appendix A: Sample Letters..197

Appendix B: Service Code Descriptions 205

Appendix C: Case Study 207

Glossary 211

Abbreviations..219

References...223

Additional Resources..227

About the Author 231

FOREWORD

Dorothy and I have known each other for over twenty-five years and have both worked in the health care field as registered nurses with expertise in different areas of practice. She certainly is a qualified expert in the field of workers compensation case management and has contributed over eighteen years of experience in this subspecialty area of nursing practice.

As a practicing University Nursing Professor, I have read this book and would recommend it to my nursing students, as well as other nursing professionals as a resource guide to understanding the specialty field of workers compensation case management. As we continue to see the changes coming about as a result of the health care reform legislation, we will also see an impact in all aspects of health care delivery in this county. As injured workers also access the healthcare system in many segments of delivery of care, case managers will continue to play an enormous part ensuring safe, and cost efficient services is provided at all levels of care. There is, therefore, a continual need that nursing professionals understand the various specialty areas of nurse practice.

A Guide to Successful Workers' Compensation Case Management is an excellent resource to bridge the knowledge gap as well as serve as an informational platform for the field of health care in general. Whether you are a case manager beginning in this field or an experienced practitioner looking to improve or regain that performance edge in representing your client's best interest to obtain specific knowledge, this guide will keep you on top of your case. This resource guide provides several interesting tools for industry case managers to use in handling that difficult case that sometimes needs an outside consult on.

There are many ways to benefit from using this resource guide because it provides you with a step-by-step plan to case management from opening to closing a case. Whether it's how to set-up a new case referral, or how to communicate with the parties to the claim, such as: the injured worker, physician, adjuster and the employer. How can a nurse remain a client advocate when hired by the claims adjuster? There have even been situations when I've asked, "How do I approach a clinical situation where there appears to be a conflict of interest in providing patient care? Where do my loyalties lie, to the hospital that hired me or to my patient?" Patient advocacy and other topics are clearly covered throughout the chapters in this book, as well as answers to those possible ethical dilemmas nurses may face in this specific industry.

This book is for those professionals who are serious about managing their cases more efficiently and effectively. It is easy to read, and adds real value to your case management success, from learning basic workers compensation case management skills to achieving ongoing success through use of proven strategies that have been the author's success story for many years. She now wants to share them with you.

– Charlene Smith, PhD, RN

PREFACE

The idea for this book, *A Guide to Successful Workers' Compensation Case Management*, began more than three years ago from my desire to write a user guide on workers' compensation case management. As I searched for books and information about this topic, I was able to locate only a few specific pages. More information is written about hospital case management as compared to workers' compensation. These findings moved me toward researching and writing my own book. There are countless books, articles, and publications written on case management. In capturing my thoughts about the differences between hospital and workers' compensation case management, I challenged myself to begin to just write. As I've learned, writing a detailed practice guide is a very time-consuming experience. I worked full-time and wrote chapters at night and on the weekends, much as I did when I was in graduate school. I have a greater appreciation now for professional writers and what it takes to achieve this level of accomplishment. Writing a book requires a lot of reading, research, and free thought processes, but most of all it requires a love for creativity. I have come to grips with the fact that whatever document my writings produce will outlive me, so I knew it had to be a work that my family could be proud of.

ACKNOWLEDGMENTS

I would like to thank my husband Don, who encouraged me to continue writing, even when I was too exhausted and wanted to give up. Appreciation also goes to my two granddaughters, whom I love dearly and am grateful for; to Alexis for creating my cover page; and to Myah, who found me writing on numerous weekends and said to me more than once, "Mommo it takes too long to write a book. I'm never going to write one."

To my daughter, Rhonda, I thank you for reviewing my documents for grammar and punctuation errors. To my son, Courtney, and my daughter-in-law Mauryo, thanks for providing moral support. So many friends and colleagues have inspired and encouraged me over the years and reviewed the manuscript for content, grammar, and accuracy. I thank you for your support and encouragement. It kept me going!

INTRODUCTION

A Guide to Successful Workers' Compensation Case Management is a resource book intended for professionals practicing in the workers' compensation industry. Case Managers, adjusters, insurers, attorneys, physicians, vocational rehabilitation specialists and employers, can stay current on state regulatory issues that affect the quality, efficiency and efficacy of your injured worker's medical care.

Prior to the existence of this reference guide, there was no quick resource to access information required by most workers' compensation professionals who practice across state lines. This guide intends to reduce the time and stress spent on conducting individual state regulatory research.

A Guide to Successful Workers' Compensation Case Management was written by a practicing case manager to share her years of experience in the field with other healthcare professionals and industry leaders. This step-by-step guide effectively represents her years of knowledge and experience in developing a successful workers' compensation professional practice model. Whether you are just starting out or are a seasoned workers' compensation professional, this book will help you take your practice to the next level.

In this copy, you will find information regarding best practices for workers' compensation professionals and easy-to-implement action plans and product examples designed to help you get from point A to point B in achieving positive outcomes.

Topics include but are not limited to:

- Defining workers' compensation case management;
- Qualifications required to become a workers' compensation case manager;
- The workers' compensation team in decision making;
- Steps to getting the injured worker back to work;
- Client advocacy in communicating with medical providers; and
- State by state guidelines on professional case management practice.

CONTINUING EDUCATION CREDITS

By purchasing this book, you are eligible to receive ten hours of continuing education credits (CE) in case management. This course will identify certain state guidelines and their impact on the practice of workers' compensation case management in rehabilitation on a state-by-state basis. Please go to www.fairnotandassociates.com for more information.

Objectives:

1. To educate CCM board certified case managers on their role and function in workers' compensation care coordination.

2. Identify activities to achieving positive return to work outcomes in managing the workers compensation case in the rehabilitation process.

3. Apply CCMC's Essential Case Management Activity Guidelines and Core Competencies of Case Management in a workers compensation setting.

4. Apply client-centered case management strategies to advocate for the injured worker in self-directed care.

5. Identify state and federal rules and regulations that affect the delivery of workers' compensation case management services.

6. Identify case outcome best practices that target a specific population such as the injured worker.

Resource Material:

This book includes a posttest for educational credit, located at www.fairnotandassociates.com.

- You may obtain 10 CE contact credit hours, which are equivalent to 50,000 words by completing a thirty-question posttest and program evaluation form located in the book appendix.

- You will have 30 multiple-choice questions provided to achieve 10 CE credit hours to be completed in one calendar year.

- Those applying for CE credit hours are required to submit their completed post-test answers, evaluation form, and purchase receipt on the website, to receive a certificate of completion.
- A pass score of 70 is required to achieve 10 contact credit hours. A certificate verifying test score and/or CE credit hours achieved will be emailed to the purchaser within one month from submission of the required documents.
- All book sales are final and book purchase may be applied for 10 CE credit hours.

Designation Statement:

This program has been approved by The Commission for Case Manager Certification to provide continuing education credit to CCM board certified case managers. The course is approved for 10 CE contact hours.

Disclaimer: The author and faculty reviewer have no financial relationships with any commercial companies in regards to this continuing education product.

Chapter 1
OVERVIEW OF CASE MANAGEMENT

The role of the workers' compensation case manager may include but is not limited to case assessment, it includes an interview with the injured worker; development, implementation and coordination of an action plan in conjunction with medical care providers and the injured worker; to evaluate medical treatment options; plan for re-entry into society; return to current employment, or a referral to vocational rehabilitation services for re-employment assessment. Simply stated, the professional case manager acts as the hub that keeps the wheel of care delivery moving in the right direction and toward the destination of achieving client-centered goals, such as maximum medical improvement (MMI).

A Guide to Successful Workers' Compensation Case Management provides a medical case management process from the perspective of a registered nurse. Workers' compensation case management is a subspecialty within the case management field. This subspecialty specifically deals with employees who have sustained a physical or emotional injury during the course of employment. The case manager's primary role is to advocate for the injured worker through compliance with the state workers' compensation laws. The goal of case management services is to return the injured worker to reasonable employment, if possible, or to restore their level of physical abilities to an optimal level of functioning.

State Regulations for Workers' Compensation Case Management

Workers' compensation is a no-fault insurance benefit covered under employment. It does not assign fault except in cases in which the employee violates safety procedures, is intoxicated, or engages in intentional personal injury activities. Most states do not recognize emotional stress as an on-the-job injury unless it is related to a work-related post-traumatic stress incident.

Workers' compensation is regulated by the laws of each state. Each state has a legislative body that determines the specific requirements for workers' compensation managed care. Each state has its own individual guidelines, rules, regulations, and qualifications. Depending on the state, the managed care provider may be a practitioner within any of these areas of clinical practice: nurses, social workers, vocational counselors, various therapists, physicians, and/or other specialty areas. Each practitioner must be licensed within each state in their specific area of practice. Many states require the practitioner providing case management services to have state-specific certification or be registered with the state prior to practicing case management. There have been several organizational initiatives to address nurse case manager practice across state lines such as the National Council of State Boards of Nursing (NCSBN), which received the support of the Case Manager Society of America (CMSA).

Nurse Licensure Compact

The Nurse Licensure Compact (NLC) Administration is a nonprofit entity established by the National Council of State Boards of Nursing (NCSBN). The general purpose of the Nurse Licensure Compact is to promote compliance with laws that govern the practice of nursing in each jurisdictional state. Its goal is to eliminate the duplication requirement of nurse licensure to practice by granting nurses the privilege of multiple state licensures. As the practice of nursing has become more mobile with the advancement of technology in communication, it has become necessary for states to become more flexible and innovative in their nurse licensure requirements. Some nurses work in the travel field, while others work as case managers. Both specialty areas of practice require nurses to work across state lines and that requires licensures in each state. A specific example are workers' compensation case managers who are licensed to practice in their state of residency but have clients who live or are treated in adjacent states. The 1997 Policy Statement by the National Council of State Boards of Nursing (NCSBN) defines "tele-nursing" as the practice of nursing by telephone and asserts that it is regulated by state boards of nursing.[1]

With the advent of advancing technology nurses are able to practice case management across state lines. Internet and intranet communication is now more accessible than ever before from remote locations. Given this greater access to communication, nurses are able to practice effectively across state lines.

The only limitation a nurse has is in having a valid nursing license for interstate practice. There continues to be an urgent need for states to ratify legislation which

---

[1] National Council of State Boards of Nursing definition of tele-nursing: the practice of nursing by telephone; regulated by state boards of nursing.

allows nurses to meet the needs of clients who may had been injured in one state but reside in another state where they are receiving medical care. Nurse case managers should be aware that even if they are providing internet or telephonic case management advice, they are practicing nursing as defined by the Nurse Practice Act and must be licensed in that state of adjudication.

One License — Twenty-Four States and Counting…

Since the NCBSN launched its campaign in 2000 to expand multistate licensure to allow for increased mobility for nurses practicing in their residential state as well as other jurisdictional states, twenty-four states have signed onto the compact. The following states are currently listed in the NLC: Arizona, Arkansas, Colorado, Delaware, Idaho, Iowa, Kentucky, Maine, Maryland, Mississippi, Missouri, Nebraska, New Hampshire, New Mexico, North Carolina, North Dakota, Rhode Island, South Carolina, South Dakota, Tennessee, Texas, Utah, Virginia, and Wisconsin.

In most states, registered nurses are considered qualified to provide case management services; however, some states require case managers to have advanced certification. The specific advanced certifications may be as a certified case manager, certified medical disability specialist, or certified rehabilitation registered nurse. Other skills and experience may be related to occupational health, rehabilitation nursing, disability management, hospital case management, or utilization management. Successful transitioning to workers' compensation case management requires the knowledge, skills, and experience in one or more of the following clinical areas: occupational rehabilitation, neurology, orthopedics, home health, emergency nursing, catastrophic or trauma case management, intensive care, or surgical and medical nursing. A registered nurse generally is required by the state board of nursing to maintain an active current license, which may require continuous education credits to meet renewal standards. Licensed professionals, specifically nurses, must have a state license for every state in which they practice. This is particularly important if the case manager is providing telephonic services that may require them to handle patients from numerous states. Even if the case manager is based in a different state, they are required to know and follow the guidelines set forth by the state of adjudication of the claim. Most states clearly denote that the case manager is the injured worker's advocate and should serve as a neutral facilitator between all parties related to the claim.

Under the workers' compensation system, case managers are responsible for addressing treatment modalities related to an on-the-job injury or a medical condition that can be correlated to the work environment. In essence, the definition of case management is broad enough to fit several areas of case management practice throughout the health and human services field. It is the case manager's responsibility to ensure that workers' compensation insurance funds are being used appropriately while managing all medically related claim activities, which take ethical considerations into account.

Ethical Guidelines

Just as case managers are responsible for coordinating an injured worker's medical care, they also are responsible for ensuring that workers' compensation insurance benefits are used only for procedures and treatments that are medically related to the worker's on-the-job injury. Carriers should be billed only for medical services related to the injury and medical necessary care that is established to aide in the injured worker's recovery. Once an injured worker has attained reasonable recovery from a work-related injury, he or she is expected to be released from medical care to return to work, by the medical provider. Injured workers who respond well to treatment modalities are deemed medically stable and are discharged from care. In some situations, injured workers are eligible for maintenance medical care; in many cases, however, the medical release will close the medical benefit obligation of the carrier to the injured worker.

Chapter 2
COORDINATED TEAM APPROACH TO WORKERS' COMPENSATION CASE MANAGEMENT

In the workers' compensation system, the professional case manager addresses the needs of individuals who have job-related illnesses, injuries, or impairments. Medical conditions may range from minor injuries or illnesses that require a minimum of intervention to more severe or even catastrophic conditions. Usually, a case manager is involved when the medical condition or other physical impairment impacts the individual's ability to perform the duties and functions of his or her job. The more serious and complex the condition is, the greater the need for care coordination by a professional case manager.

An effective approach to workers' compensation case management requires a team of skilled professionals who are committed to working collectively to achieve the same objective: the injured worker's recovery and eventual return to work. The typical care team consists of the treating medical provider, case managers (employed by the workers' compensation carrier or self-insured employer), the claims adjuster, and the employer. Depending on the severity or complexity of the case other professionals may be involved, such as specialty physicians and clinicians, a hospital-based or home health case manager, occupational or physical therapists, and vocational rehabilitation counselors to expedite care, as well as a safe recovery for the injured worker.

The team approach has been recognized as an effective means to improve efficiency within the health care system. The Institute of Medicine, in its groundbreaking report, "Crossing the Quality Chasm," emphasized the creation of patient-centered care teams (Institutes of Medicine, 2010.) Greater cooperation and collaboration among health care teams is essential to overcome the fragmentation that has riddled the system when professionals operate in silos, focusing only on their individual roles in care delivery.

One case management practice setting that has historically utilized a team-approach is workers' compensation. Because of the many parties and stakeholders involved, a team approach is essential to achieving a quality outcome while containing costs. At the center of that team is the professional case manager who coordinates the full spectrum of care, based on the client's needs, while operating within the regulatory framework of state-mandated workers' compensation systems.

As various models of care are advanced, the workers' compensation case management approach serves as an example for managing complex cases involving numerous parties and stakeholders, with an emphasis on efficiency, quality, and client-centered goals.

The case manager's ability to establish a professional relationship, and share information is the hallmark for achieving a successful case outcome during interactions with the workers' compensation team. The case manager is required to conduct continuous collaboration on many topics that affect case outcomes. Information regarding changes in the injured worker's medical condition should be shared with the team members on an ongoing basis. The changes communicated to the team may be as simple as adding a new medication or as complex as surgical intervention.

The Team Approach to Shared Decision Making

The Case Manager

To effectively communicate with the team members involved in a work-related injury claim, the case manager should understand not only his or her own role, but also the explicit details about the referral assignment as well as the responsibilities of all team members.

The case manager assumes the role as an advocate for care coordination by establishing effective communication with all parties in order to manage the overall outcome of the injured worker's case. Following the case referral assignment, the case manager has to establish relationships among all parties, which is an essential part of the case management process. Upon receiving a referral for case management services for an injured worker, the case manager should contact all involved parties to the claim to explain the case manager's role, establish expectations, and ascertain the team's preferred communication method, which may be via telephone, email, written reports, or a combination of these.

The case manager is obligated to comply with all state regulations that affect communication with all parties to the claim. Many states require written notice be given to the injured worker, advising that case management has been retained. In addition to contacting the injured worker by phone, the case manager should follow up by sending an introductory letter informing the injured worker about the purpose of case management and his or her rights under workers' compensation statues. The injured worker should be informed that medical information including the case manager's report will be sent to the other involved parties.

The case manager should be aware that some states prohibit *ex parte* communications. Ex parte is a legal term that basically means one-sided communication. An example of ex parte communication would be if a case manager met with the treating medical providers in the absence of the injured worker or his or her representative. If the injured worker is present, then no ex parte violation is applicable.

Although not every state has specific rules for case manager communication, many states do, and it is the case manager's responsibility to understand each specific state's regulations when providing case management services. If the injured worker or employer/insurer has retained an attorney, depending on the state regulations, it would be prudent for the case manager to speak with the attorney on record prior to communication with the injured worker. In some states, the injured worker's attorney may have the right to limit or disallow some or all communication with certain parties involved with the claim. After establishing the preferred communication mechanism for each party, the case manager may then begin actively reviewing information about the injury, medical treatment, and physical restrictions, and may communicate with all the involved parties throughout the life of the case.

The case manager should provide written or verbal updates throughout the case assignment until the claim is closed for case management services. A claim may be closed for case management, but may continue to remain open until the claim adjuster is able to reach a claim settlement. With most referred assignments, the case manager is expected to complete an initial report within forty-eight hours of the initial injured worker's interview. An initial report, a monthly medical status interim report and a final closure report, are all required written documents to be submitted to the adjuster, and are also considered requirements until conclusion of the case assignment. Depending on state requirements, the attorneys also may request a copy of the monthly written report. The case manager should be aware that the referring agency may restrict or limit the case manager's ability to forward documents to certain parties to the claim based on case litigation; which may include all verbal and written material. Therefore, parties to the claim to whom communication is privileged should establish communication standards at the time of case manager referral.

Documentation of communication is important for continuity of care and for compliance with state legal regulations. The case manager should document all conversations, time and expense work activities, and all interactions conducted on behalf of the injured worker in the case file. Each injured worker should have a confidential file in which all documentation, medical records, reports, and written correspondence are stored in a locked file cabinet. Often, the injured worker's employer will have specific account instructions outlining the expected report format and injured worker contact information. Most companies now have computer systems to store information electronically, for case managers who work in a corporate type setting. When documenting communication, the case manager should write a brief summary of each communication and the actions implemented. The documentation should represent clear and accurate case facts. The case manager should avoid documenting anything that could be construed as bias, such as personal opinionated statements about the injured worker or other parties to the claim. The documentation should not include any perceived opinions of the case manager. The case manager may document exact quotes received from a party to the claim that may impact the injured worker's outcome. The documentation should represent an accurate summary of the case manager's work activities based on factual case accounts as all documents are subject to subpoena and may be used in court cases.

The Injured Worker

The injured worker is the employee who sustained an on-the-job injury during the course of employment. The injured worker may experience feelings of helplessness and anxiety resulting from a work injury. Often, the injured worker may believe that his or her employment status may be jeopardized as a result of the injury claim.

It is important for the injured worker to understand that the OSHA Act of 1970 protects workers who complain to their employer, the Occupational Safety & Health Administration (OSHA), or other governmental agency about unsafe or unhealthy working conditions in the workplace or environmental problems. According to OSHA, employees cannot be transferred, denied a raise, fired, have work hours reduced, or be punished in any other way because they used any right given to them under the OSHA Act.

Injured workers often are referred to as "claimants." Claimant is a legal term meaning the person or the party who makes a claim for benefits or compensation. Workers' compensation is very different from major medical insurance, so the injured worker may not understand his or her rights under workers' compensation statues. The injured worker may need to be directed to the adjuster or employer in regard to benefits and compensability of the claim as the case manager is not qualified to discuss monetary and compensability issues. Although the case manager is not responsible for discussing the injured workers' benefits, he or she should be aware that the injured worker typically is compensated for time off work, which can create secondary gain issues. Secondary gains may be identified as the injured worker who enjoys the personal attention received by his injury or may use the on the job injury as an opportunity to benefit financially so he or she may engage in symptom magnification to prolong medical care.

The Employer

The employer in a workers' compensation injury claim is the employer on record that has accepted the work-related injury as its responsibility. It is important to understand that the injured worker may not be employed by the same employer when the file is referred. The employer listed as party to the claim, remains as party to the claim until the claim is settled by the adjuster. An injured worker may resign or be terminated from employment with the employer on record, but would still be eligible to receive medical benefits as provided by state law. When the case manager receives the referral, the employer on record may be contacted to discuss the status of the case if allowed by the referring source. Consideration should be given to the discussion of the work-place safety issues, which may vary depending on the employer size, industry, and state location. The employer's goal and return to work programs may differ depending on how their on-the-job safety risk program is designed and administered. Some employers may embrace the case manager's efforts in achieving a transitional-duty job return to work status for the injured worker. Other employers may view this type of return to work job assignment as encroaching upon federal disability statutes that address the employer's responsibility in providing permanent reasonable work accommodations, which may not be applicable in this instance, as this reference is for temporary work accommodations.

The best way for an employer to achieve a cost savings on their workers' compensation claims is to take charge and become an active participant, by establishing a return to work program that keeps the injured worker engaged in their job. The employer must be involved in all essential case management functions by working closely with the workers' compensation team during the injured worker's medical recovery.

The Adjuster

A workers' compensation claims adjuster is responsible for handling workers' compensation claims and file management. Once a claim is filed for an injured worker, the adjuster is responsible for determining whether the claim is work-related and compensable. If the claim is accepted, the adjuster refers the file for case management in order to coordinate medical care for the injured worker by approving and authorizing treatment, surgery, medications, appointments, and all other medically necessary services to promote recovery. The adjuster reimburses for case-related bills, including medical and indemnity payments to the injured worker for the time he or she is unable to work, payments to doctors and pharmacies, payments to attorneys for consulting and providing legal advice, and any other payments that may occur within the scope of the claim. The adjuster issues legal notices as required by the state to inform the injured worker of his or her rights and benefits entitled under workers' compensation insurance coverage. The workers' compensation claims adjuster works with the employer and the injured worker to expedite care and to achieve a return to work (RTW) release, even if it is to a transitional-duty position.

Many adjusters do not have medical education or training, may not understand the injured worker's medical records, and may rely on medical interpretation from the case manager. For example, what does a positive test result mean? In certain circumstances, the meaning is totally different to a layperson than to an experienced medical case manager. The case manager is a valuable resource to the adjuster in interpreting medical documentation and in maneuvering through a complex medical health care system to obtain the appropriate care for the injured worker.

The Attorney

Case managers often will receive a referral assignment with attorney representation noted on the file. The attorney involved in the case typically is a plaintiff's attorney. Injured workers tend to contact attorneys to represent them because they lack an understanding of their rights under the workers' compensation system. The injured worker may also believe that he or she can sue their employer, but they cannot; the workers' compensation law is the exclusive remedy for addressing coverage for an on- the-job injury. The injured worker can only receive redress for those statutes legislated in the state workers' compensation act.

When a case manager receives a referred injured worker's case that has a plaintiff attorney representation, it is the case manager's responsibility to contact the plaintiff's attorney before contacting the injured worker. The plaintiff's attorney is the legal representative of the injured worker; therefore all contact and case information must be routed through the plaintiff's attorney. The regulations required for attorney contact are listed under the state's workers' compensation guidelines. Some case managers may err in judgment if they assume that attorney contact is an option; in most states it is not, especially if the attorney is the injured worker's representative of record.

Case managers should contact the attorney on record within one business day of receiving the referral to acknowledge the case management assignment, as requested by the referring party, and based on the state regulatory guidelines, to request consent to have direct contact with the injured worker.

If the plaintiff attorney consents to contact with the injured worker, the case manager may proceed with the initial injured worker contact. If consent to contact the injured employee is denied, the case manager should notify the adjuster and employer. Case managers should submit a written request to the plaintiff's attorney requesting approval to contact the client after verbal contact is made. The attorney's response should be documented in the case file. In most states, written attorney refusal disallows case managers from contacting the client. However, some states do allow case managers who are employed by a third party administrator (TPA) or managed care organization (MCO) to contact medical providers because they are payers of the claim.

In situations where attorney consent is established, the case manager is encouraged to collaborate with all parties in advocating for the rights of the injured worker. The case manager's role should include ongoing communication providing all parties with medical records and reports. Communication also may include responding to subpoenas and depositions or appearing in court to testify. The case manager's testimony should be unbiased—representing the facts of the case without undue influence from any party.

The Medical Provider

The role of the medical provider is to treat the injured worker's medical condition, to monitor and prevent complications, and to gain the injured worker's compliance with the prescribed treatment plan.

An ongoing medical provider's assessment is to evaluate the injured worker for temporary or permanent physical capabilities and limitations. It is important to remember that physical limitations are applicable not only to the injured worker's ability to function at work but are applicable to daily living activities. When the case manager addresses physical restrictions with the medical provider, it is critical that the medical provider address not only the medical findings but the injured worker's understanding, in order to prevent any setbacks during recovery.

The case manager generally will be responsible for coordinating, scheduling, and attending physician's appointments with the injured worker. The case manager should dress professionally and maintain professional communication at all times. Case managers are responsible for establishing a collaborative relationship with medical providers and their staff. Case managers should present themselves as the advocate for the injured worker, not the representative for the insurance carrier.

When communicating with the medical provider, the case manager should understand what is meant by reasonable and medical necessity. Medical necessity should translate into what is medically necessary for the injured worker's recovery. The injured worker is entitled to reasonable medically necessary care. However, every treatment or item the medical provider orders may not meet this category criteria. It is the case manager's responsibility to challenge the medical provider if treatments are ordered that are not essential to recovery. By the same token, there are treatments and tests that may benefit the injured worker and should be included to expedite recovery;

this, too, should cause the case manager to guide the medical provider's decision. The case manager should understand that higher medical cost up-front often saves cost over the life of the case.

The case manager should address the injured worker's anticipated return to work and physical restrictions when meeting with the medical provider. It is challenging for a case manager to balance advocacy in pursuing conversations in the presence of the injured worker. The main focus of the conversation with the medical provider should center on care and the best medical option for the injured worker's recovery. A delay or failure to return an injured worker to productive employment may not be the best medical, psychosocial, or financial option for the injured worker.

Once the medical provider has addressed physical limitations, the case manager can then provide the medical provider's recommendations to the employer to determine if the employer can accommodate the injured worker's specific physical limitations with a transitional-duty-work position. At each subsequent conference, the case manager and medical provider should address any changes to the injured worker's physical restrictions in an effort to prevent the injured worker from further injury, and to ensure the safety of the injured worker and other employees working in the same environment.

After physical restrictions are determined by the medical provider, the case manager should provide the restrictions to the employer. The employer will determine whether the restrictions can be accommodated. The case manager's responsibility is only to facilitate an appropriate medical RTW release based on the injured worker's physical abilities and limitations. To accomplish a successful transitioning back to work, the case manager must first obtain a signed transitional job description from the injured worker's employer and obtain a medical provider's signature that the injured worker is capable of performing the task as outlined. It is the employer's responsibility to accept or reject the medical provider's recommendations for return to work. The case manager must be knowledgeable that some states require that the injured worker or their attorney review the job description prior to the medical provider's decision.

Chapter 3
WORKERS' COMPENSATION CASE MANAGER QUALIFICATIONS

Case managers are required to maintain compliance with their state boards' of Nursing Practice Act and their certification board's ethical code of conduct, as well as the state workers' compensation board's regulations for practice in each state they provide case management services.

Case managers are also required to have experience in assessing an injured worker's medical condition and psychosocial needs that affect the ability to work based on workers' compensation statutes and state jurisdiction of the claim. Case managers coordinate care whether it's medical, vocational, or psychiatric to meet the injured worker's health care needs. In addition, case managers promote available resources that provide quality cost-effective outcomes and that lead to a successful return to work plan.

Case managers must have previous clinical experience and medical case management experience that support their knowledge in working with healthcare providers, vendors and community resources to coordinate the injured worker's needs in scheduling medical services, providing adaptive home devices, home health care, and RTW initiatives.

Case managers traditionally handle lost-time cases as well as medical only cases that require transitional work duty implementation. This process requires that case managers maintain open communication and collaboration with the injured worker, employer, and medical provider to analyze the next course in medical treatment options.

The following are typical industry-accepted qualification criteria for the workers' compensation case manager:
- A degree from an accredited nursing school maintaining an unrestricted registered nursing license;
- A minimum of two years nursing experience in a related industry practice area;
- Ability to practice independently, to think critically and analytically, to solve problems, and to set priorities;
- Ability to communicate effectively in verbal and written forms.

Experience/Training

In the practice of case management, a core knowledge and experience level forms the skills required to optimize the worker's compensation case outcome. Some core knowledge will be in the areas of medical injury management, having people skills, understanding state legislation related to work safety and workers' compensation regulations, incorporated into an ability to practice independently. The following list of experience and training will transition well into workers' compensation case management:

1. Certified case manager
2. Medical case management
3. Care coordinator
4. Occupational health nurse
5. Workers' compensation and/or rehabilitation nursing
6. Writing case management action plans and reports
7. Working with an occupational health medical team
8. Medical insurance case management
9. Vocational rehabilitation case management

Case Manager Certifications

Some states require that case managers have some type of certification, such as Certified Case Manager (CCM), Certified Disability Medical Specialist (CDMS), Certified Occupational Health Nurse (COHN) and/or Certified Rehabilitation Registered Nurse (CRRN) designations. Many employers will reimburse qualified case managers for the cost to maintain certification. In addition to certification, an on-site case manager also will be required to have a valid driver's license and a vehicle with insurance coverage because frequent travel is involved. Some employer organizations may provide a vehicle, as well as vehicle insurance coverage for the case manager to use for on-site visits. Case managers are required to maintain their professional license and certification through continuing education courses.

Essential Activities of Case Managers

When a case manager receives a referral, he or she should interview the injured worker by assessing the reported body part injured, review the worker's symptoms, review the medical records, and consult with the medical provider. After the case manager completes the initial injured worker's interview assessment, the information is then available to develop an action plan with short and long-term goals to ultimately return the injured worker back to gainful employment. It should be noted that return to gainful employment may not necessarily be with the employer on record.

Elements of successful workers' compensation Case management include the following: [2]

Assessment
Review the medical records to collect in-depth information; interview the injured worker; consult with the treating physician (s); secure authorization and consent from the injured worker; notify the referral source; and complete a comprehensive assessment.

Planning
Develop an action plan that addresses symptoms, prognosis, and progress toward recovery and return to work; obtain a job description from the employer; submit a state-man-dated case management plan and document the injured worker's progress.

Implementation
Monitor the medical treatment plan; maintain open communication with providers and request second medical opinions if progress is slow or impaired. Implement actions and interventions that will lead to accomplishing the goals set forth in the case management plan.

Coordination
Facilitate ancillary treatment and care and coordinate medical management, physical therapy, occupational therapy, home health services, and durable medical equipment, as needed.

---

[2] Consonery-Fairnot, Dorothy, "Enhancing the Team Approach to Care with Professional Case Management." *Professional Case Management*. 17. no. 1 (2011): 29-30.

Monitoring

Ensure injured workers attendance at all appointments; maintain medication compliance; and make sure all providers have shared information.

Evaluation

Evaluate and document the injured worker's progress toward recovery; update the treatment plan; and analyze treatments versus progress versus cost to determine the best treatment alternatives.

Outcomes

Make frequent assessments of action plan items to achieve case closure, track costs, and complete cost savings report to document if case management interventions were effective and beneficial to the injured worker's recovery.

General

Ensure compliance with all workers' compensation laws and statues; maintain an accessible database of all local medical providers in the community service area; conduct research on emerging medical treatments and advancements in care; and maintain ethical practice standards and injured worker's confidentiality.

Chapter 4
ORGANIZATIONS THAT REFER TO CASE MANAGEMENT SERVICES

The types of organizations that refer injured workers for case management services may include but are not limited to medical and workers' compensation insurance companies, third-party administrators (TPAs), self-insured employers, independent claims adjustment companies, managed care organizations (MCOs), health maintenance organizations (HMOs), and various federal and state programs.

Referral Triggers

Case management is considered an adjunct resource service that is provided by a professional case manager to coordinate an injured worker's medical care across a continuum of care needs. It also has a thirty year history in controlling medical cost and in providing quality care outcomes through client advocacy, which leads to better client satisfaction. A number of outcome expectations on the part of the referral source may lead to case manager referrals, including:

- The severity of alleged injury does not appear to correlate with the incident of injury as reported.
- During the course of treatment, the injured worker introduces several unrelated conditions and symptoms, not related to the initial injury.
- The physician is treating the patient for medical conditions, such as diabetes mellitus and/or hypertension, unrelated to the current treatment plan.
- The injured worker is receiving several treatment modalities from multiple medical providers.
- The injured worker is receiving lengthy chiropractic treatment without justification that the treatment offers any benefit or improvement to his or her condition.
- The injured worker has received a permanent disability rating that cannot be correlated to the stated injury or identified symptoms.
- The medical provider treatment regimen does not appear to be medically necessary based on the injured worker's stated injury.
- The claim exposure reflects a catastrophic injury and is expected to be a high-volume cost claim.

The Referral Process

Immediately upon receipt of a referral, the case manager should begin analyzing the patient's medical and demographic information regarding the nature of the injury, prior to communicating with the injured worker. The case manager's role is to provide consultative care coordination services to the injured worker, employer, and adjuster on how best to utilize appropriate medical care. Failure to timely refer a file to a case manager increases file expenses, prolongs treatment, and often leads to delayed recovery and unsatisfactory outcomes. To complete the referral process, the case manager should obtain the following claim data:

1. The injured worker's name, demographic information, and contact numbers, which are crucial for purposes of communication.

2. Date of birth, social security number, and photo identification, all of which are generally required by medical providers to identify the injured worker.

3. The state of adjudication to ensure that proper regulations are followed. The injured worker's state of residency is not necessarily the state of the claim adjudication; a variety of reasons may influence which state is selected as the state of adjudication (e.g., the employee may have been injured in a state other than his residency).

4. The specific injury sustained by the injured worker. The employer is generally only responsible for funding medical services that restore the injured worker to their pre-injury state. The case manager should make every effort to limit coordination of care to the specific body part(s) injured during the course of employment. The injured worker may require other medical treatment that may necessitate the use of his or her major medical insurance or other funding types.

5. The claim number, which is typically requested by medical providers; therefore, it is important to obtain it in order to make coordination of care easier.

6. The specific job description held by the injured worker at the time of injury, which is essential to developing an RTW action plan.

Types of Workers' Compensation Case Management Services

The type of case management services requested by the referral source will determine the role the case manager will play in the claims process. The roles of workers' compensation case management services typically requested are telephonic and on-site. In addition to the two roles are types of case management service levels that may fall under on-site care, such as: full, task, medical only, and/or catastrophic case assignments.

Telephonic Case Management

The telephonic case manager (TCM) provides treatment protocols per telephone or e-mail to coordinate medical care as follows:

1. Collaborate with all parties by phone or e-mail the specific role of case management and to routinely update involved parties.
2. Collaborate with the treating medical providers to obtain treatment plan.
3. Monitor and review the treatment plan to ensure it is within industry norms.
4. Assist with the coordination of prescribed medical treatments.
5. Coordinate RTW by discerning physical restrictions and determining if the employer can accommodate.
6. Maintain communication with the injured worker to monitor medical progress.
7. Document the case file per state protocol, including compliance with state regulations and/or employer account instructions.
8. Complete any state required forms as delineated by the state of adjudication.

Managing the Medical Only Case

Medical-only claims are identified as minor injuries that may or may not include lost time from work or limited to seven days from the workplace. Some cases are considered medical only without lost time from work; the injured worker may be working a transitional-duty job (transitional-duty is work activities that meet a medical work restriction outside the regular employee's job description). To effectively assess and manage medical only cases, the case manager should be aware of all work restrictions or limitations placed on the injured worker by the medical provider. The case manager should be in communication with the employer to determine if there is an appropriate transitional-duty job available for the injured worker that will not further delay or hinder the medical recovery process. The case manager should communicate with the claims adjuster as to the status of the medical only claim because an out of work status will require the adjuster to implement indemnity benefits.

A case manager may be assigned to medical only cases to evaluate the need for continued medical management when the injured worker is on transitional-duty and continues to receive medical care to facilitate progression to full duty. In situations where the adjuster receives information from the medical provider that an injured worker is noncompliant with medical protocol, the case manager may request a second medical opinion or an independent medical evaluation (IME).

Any decision of the case manager that may result in increasing the claim cost should be discussed with the adjuster before any action is taken. If the adjuster concurs that a second opinion or IME is indicated, the case manager usually is responsible for scheduling the medical evaluation and may be requested to attend. Because the role of the case manager is to ensure that the injured worker is receiving the appropriate medical care based on medical diagnosis—which may require other medical opinions— there is no conflict of interest in scheduling further medical evaluations in order to obtain a definitive treatment plan.

The following minor injuries may be considered as medical only claims:

- First-degree burns covering less than 10 percent of the body
- Superficial lacerations/contusions
- Minor animal/human bites
- Superficial foreign object in eye
- Corneal abrasion
- Superficial/abrasion skin injury
- Sprains/strains

Lost-Time Claims

In general, if an injured worker is off work for seven days or longer due to a covered injury or occupational disease, the claim is considered a lost-time claim. If 14 or more days are missed due to a covered injury or illness, the injured worker may be compensated for the entire period of time disabled from work as a result of the injury or occupational disease specific to state guidelines.

Task Assignment

A task assignment usually represents a one-time specific case management activity, which may be to attend a physician appointment for a second opinion or an independent medical evaluation or to obtain medical records to schedule a special procedure, or surgical intervention. The case manager will receive a written referral request from the referring source that outlines all case manager task activities expected to be accomplished during the task assignment.

Task assignments usually close within four to six weeks. If the case assignment exceeds this time frame, the adjuster should be contacted to determine if a continued task assignment is warranted. The task activities must be written into a formal report format to include a comprehensive interview assessment of the injured worker's diagnosis, prognosis, medical treatment plan, work status, and future treatment and/or future surgeries. Once the task activities listed in the referral document has been completed by the case manager, a task report should be completed and the file closed unless otherwise directed by the referral source.

On-site Case Management

Case managers provide medical care coordination for injured workers to facilitate appropriate medical care that allows them to reach their optimum level of functional independence and quality of life. To accomplish care coordination, the case manager should incorporate the Commission for Case Manager Certification's "Essential Activities of Case Management," which is a seven-step approach to obtaining required information that can be applied not only during the initial injured worker's interview, but throughout the continuum of care process (see Chapter 3). On-site case management may take a few months or several years to achieve a successful outcome, depending on the nature of the injury (such as with the catastrophic case management file).

Catastrophic Case Management

Cases designated as "catastrophic" must meet a specific diagnosis, or an anticipated financial exposure, to satisfy this state designation. Many states have an accepted list of diagnoses as the standard for identifying a catastrophic case, such as:

- Spinal cord injuries involving severe paralysis
- Severe burns affecting 25 percent of the whole body
- Severe brain injuries or closed head injuries
- Industrial blindness
- Massive organ injuries
- Amputations involving loss of use of an extremity

In addition to meeting the state diagnoses designation, other employer or the insurer's criteria may be used, such as: referral assignments that specify that a case manager is to make a same-day hospital visit, referrals based on an injured worker's admission into a critical care unit, or referrals based on anticipated lengthy hospital stays.

Catastrophic (CAT) Case Management Process

Catastrophic work-related injuries can be life threatening events that may involve total disability or a lesser level of care requiring medical treatment over an extended period of time. It may take years for catastrophic injuries to resolve because of the ongoing medical care that is required. These injuries not only affect the injured workers, but also place serious stress on the injured worker's family who may spend years providing custodial care and emotional assistance.

The case management process involves a proactive approach to care coordination that includes continual assessing, planning, implementing, coordinating, monitoring, and evaluating medical care in order to achieve a positive case outcome. The case manager should be knowledgeable and experienced in the operations of the healthcare system to coordinate care of this severe nature. Mismanagement of a catastrophic case can result in eruptible harm to the injured worker and may be very costly to the insurer.

The case manager should be involved in every aspect of care to ensure that all levels of care delivery are coordinated throughout the process until case closure is achieved. Continuous ongoing collaboration and documentation of case activities are crucial in care coordination for catastrophic injury cases. Achieving the highest level of case management success is accomplished through a shared team approach to problem solving in delivery of care (see Chapter 2, "The Team Approach to Shared Decision Making"). Each state has specific requirements for documentation of catastrophic cases, but generally most states require the case manager to provide a verbal and written report following the initial contact made with the injured worker, hospital professionals, or medical provider during the initial and subsequent hospital visits. All documentation should include a review of the hospital medical records that indicate the injured worker's level of care is appropriate based on the stated diagnosis. Any changes in the injured worker's medical condition should be immediately communicated to the adjuster and employer, who are responsible for the claim benefits.

The following are examples of changes in the injured worker's medical condition, but this is not an all-inclusive list:
- Medical classification or level of care
- Medically induced comas
- Serious medical complications
- Scheduled surgery
- Major medication changes
- Discharge date
- Return to work (RTW) status
- Maximum medical improvement (MMI)
- Transfer from hospital to another facility for rehabilitation or other care

Chapter 5

THE INITIAL INJURED WORKERS' INTERVIEW PROCESS

Prior to the initial injured worker's interview, the case manager should conduct a review of the medical records and consult with the adjuster and treating medical provider to establish the factual information related to the case. The case manager will be responsible for formulating an RTW action plan by analyzing all of the gathered information inclusive of the injured worker's interview in order to write the initial and subsequent reports.

Meeting with the injured worker at the treating physician's office is the most appropriate setting for this interview because most on-site case management assignments require an interview of the injured worker as well as a conference with the worker's treating medical provider. If the case manager's initial interview will be delayed outside the specific state number of day's protocol, the injured worker's interview may be conducted by telephone, in a public setting, or at the injured worker's home. Some injured workers may avoid scheduling a meeting in their home because they may question the case manager's motive or relationship with the insurance carrier or employer.

If the case manager cannot conduct an initial on-site interview to meet the referral timeline, a telephone interview can be conducted instead to obtain all required information by using a comprehensive medical history assessment format. A sample interview questionnaire guideline is provided in this chapter. Case managers should be respectful of the injured worker's ethnicity and religious beliefs when asking personal questions in order to avoid offending the injured worker.

During the interview process, the injured worker should be asked to describe his or her symptoms and how the injury occurred. Asking open-ended questions is the appropriate communication technique to use when conducting client interviews. The injured worker's answers to all interview questions should be recorded as factual information, without interjecting any subjective opinions. Recording exact statements makes for best practice in legal documentation. Keep in mind that all case manager records are legal documents and subject to subpoena.

Case managers are able to empower injured workers through advocacy and by providing medical literature that details their medical condition, which will assist them in making informed medical decisions. Case managers should ensure that injured workers understand their diagnosis and treatment plan. It is important to allow injured workers to express thoughts on their medical condition and to access their level of satisfaction with their medical progress. Injured workers are more likely to adhere to medical protocol that meets their ethnic and religious value system.

It also is important to inform injured workers that their participation in the case management process is voluntary in most states, but this process can assist them in making informed decisions regarding their health care needs. However, some states require mandatory case management services as seen in catastrophic cases. A brief medical and vocational history in conjunction with a discussion regarding the injured worker's current RTW abilities may be appropriate during the initial interview.

During the interview, it should be noted whether the injured worker is cooperative and willing to make plans to return to work. Inform the injured worker that his or her help is needed in developing an appropriate RTW action plan, and that you will collaborate with them throughout the process. Let the injured worker know that you will respect his or her decision even if that decision is not to return to work.

The initial interview and assessment form should include:

- Referral company
- Case manager
- Contact information
- Date of visit
- Date of report
- Injured worker demographics
- Injured worker's name
- Social security number
- Telephone, address, and e-mail address
- Date of birth
- Occupation
- Employer
- Interview site

- Attempt to accommodate the needs of the injured worker (The medical provider's office is the most used site for meeting with the injured worker and medical provider.)
- Physical description of injured worker
- Note any identifiable abnormalities, such as gait, height, weight, appearance, scars, right- or left-hand dominance
- Social history
- Marital status
- Spouse's occupation
- Family status, including number of children
- Other support network—Indicate which family member will support the injured worker during long-term recovery or surgery.
- Ask and note if the injured worker has symptoms of depression
- Document any psychiatric history and use of psychiatric medications
- If the injured worker is not working, ask how she is spending her time
- Observe if the injured worker's stated physical limitations appear consistent with his diagnosis and symptoms
- Ask if the injured worker plans to return to work at her pre-injury job
- Ask about hobbies or social activities that may have potential for skills transfer
- Ask if the injured worker has a computer and how skilled he is in using it

Medical history
- Ask the injured worker to describe the nature of the injury.
- Ask the injured worker to explain his perception of his medical status in order to determine his understanding of his condition and prognosis.
- Document the medical provider's treatment care plan and RTW plans.
- List the current injured worker's symptoms and if there is symptom relief with medical care.
- Determine whether there is observable and medical evidence of functional impairment.
- Current medical treatment
- Gather medical provider and specialist contact information. Document if these providers communicate with each other regarding the case.
- Assess medication usage and the injured worker's understanding of medication, dosage, and the condition for which it is used.

- Ask the injured worker how quickly she is progressing through her current medical condition.
- Ask the injured worker to describe her physical strengths and limitations.

Vocational assessment
- Determine the injured worker's educational history, including the highest degree or grade level achieved, academic/trade school major, and attendance dates.
- Note any professional certificates, certifications, licenses, or affiliations and whether they are current.
- Ask about what the injured worker enjoyed most and least about his job.
- Ask the injured worker about his feelings regarding his previous employer.
- Ask the injured worker about past accomplishments (social, work, other).
- Ask about hobbies and interests.
- Identify if the injured worker has job-related transferable skills.
- Obtain a copy of the injured worker's resume or assist in developing one.

Upon completion, the injured worker's interview should result in the case manager's ability to:

- Identify the injured worker's medical treatment and RTW needs.
- Correlate the injured worker's injury with symptoms.
- Identify safety issues related to the injury.
- Identify barriers related to RTW.
- Educate the injured worker regarding his treatment plan and prognosis.
- Identify any pre-existing medical conditions.
- Identify any transferable job skills.
- Assess the injured worker's desire to return to work.
- Secure a signed medical authorization and consent form.

During the on-site interview, the case manager should obtain a signed consent from the injured worker that covers an agreement for voluntary case management services—if indicated by state statutes—as well as consent for release of medical records. The case manager should explain to the injured worker that written consent allows all parties to work together and share medical information in order to expedite coordination of medical care.

If an injured worker's medical condition limits the performance of essential job functions, the employer is obligated under the Americans with Disabilities Act (ADA) to consider reasonable accommodations that would allow the injured worker to return to work.

If an injured worker is unable to return to his present job or has a permanent impairment preventing him from seeking other employment, he may qualify for state, private, or third-party assisted vocational rehabilitation services. Case managers are responsible for knowing the state's workers' compensation guidelines regarding vocational rehabilitation requirements.

Case managers should be aware that injured workers are often released and returned to work prior to reaching maximum medical improvement (MMI) through transitional-duty or alternative duty jobs. Many case managers are assigned to the file until the injured worker has no further medical care needs, not just an MMI rating. Employers today are proactive in establishing special account instructions to ensure that their injured workers receive timely and appropriate medical care, and are encouraged to use case managers to facilitate appropriate return to work.

Over the years, employers have used statistics to validate the notion that the longer an injured worker remains unproductive, the more likely he is to not return to his pre-injury job. For this reason, case managers play a vital role in identifying ways to modify jobs to facilitate an early return to work.

Case managers who are knowledgeable of the workers' compensation system, as well as the healthcare system, and are in a unique position to identify any obstacles that could delay medical recovery. In addition to those skills, case managers are familiar with the job setting and the physical job demands required of the injured worker. Case managers should be familiar with the injured worker's job responsibilities in order to identify options and present those options to the treating medical provider during the initial and subsequent consultations. This type of collaborative communication with the medical provider creates credibility of the case manager's opinions regarding the injured worker's treatment plan and capacity to return to work.

If the employer fails to provide the case manager with RTW options, the case manager is free to discuss the injured worker's work restrictions with the adjuster. The adjuster can offer advice to the employer in support of the case manager's RTW plan. These interactions demonstrate shared team decision making in care coordination.

Establishing an Effective Case Manager Interview Checklist

The workers' compensation case manager should use the initial interview session as an opportunity to educate the injured worker as well as an opportunity to obtain all pertinent information necessary to medically manage the case. The following are suggestions for educating the injured worker while gathering and assessing information during the initial interview:

- Provide the injured worker with contact information and explain the case manager's role as an advocate for them.
- Provide the injured worker with the treating physician's contact information and hours of operation.
- Explain to the injured worker that in the event of an emergency to dial 911 or report to the nearest emergency facility.
- Educate the injured worker regarding legal rights under the state's workers' compensation guidelines. Most states have pamphlets at no cost that can be given to the injured worker.
- Explain why completing the injured worker's demographic information, is important; full legal name, correct address, zip code, and telephone number is required.
- Explain that you must secure a signature for the medical authorization form, which must be signed giving consent for voluntary case management services and medical release of information, based on state workers' compensation guidelines. The injured worker's signature enables the case manager to obtain necessary medical information to manage the case and allows the claims adjuster to pay the bills.
- Instruct the injured worker to have the treating physician complete the medical treatment plan and related return to work status in circumstances when the case manager is not present at the physician appointment.
- Instruct the injured worker that, as case manager, you will be attending the initial and subsequent medical provider appointments to assist in meeting medical goals.

- Instruct the injured worker that the medical provider will be requested to complete certain work status and work restriction forms and those forms will be provided to the adjuster and to the employer.
- Instruct the injured worker that it will be up to the employer to provide reasonable work-related accommodations based on the medical provider's recommendations.
- Inform the injured worker that the information gathered will be entered into the written action plan goals and objectives.

Case Manager Action Plan for Return to Work

The case manager has the responsibility to ensure that the appropriate medical release has been obtained from the treating medical providers. In preparation for recommending that an injured worker be returned to work on transitional-duty, the case manager will review the job description and analyze the medical restrictions of the specific job to determine its appropriateness for the work setting. The case manager should keep in mind that the greatest predictor of returning an injured worker to work is when the injured worker feels ready to return to work.

The job description and medical restrictions provide a framework for analyzing the tasks and physical demands the injured worker may experience, which is the basic reference for developing an appropriate transitional-duty job. When an injured worker is ready to return to work, medical clearance for work with defined capabilities and restrictions is obtained from the medical provider. The capabilities and restrictions are communicated to the employer by the injured worker, case manager, adjuster, or medical provider. The employer develops the transitional-duty job list based on the capabilities or restrictions received from the medical provider. The case manager then reviews and approves the transitional-duty job description prior to submitting the plan to the physician for approval. The case manager also submits a transitional-duty job description to the medical provider in order to facilitate a release to return to work with an accompanied request for recommended restrictions and capabilities.

An RTW action plan includes determining:
- The injured worker's restrictions and physical capabilities as identified by the medical provider.
- The transitional-duty job's return to work date.

- The work schedule and full duty progression plan.
- The name of the employer contact responsible for monitoring the injured worker while on transitional-duty.
- The RTW date identified by the employer.
- Whether the employer has made a job offer to the injured worker.

Monitoring Transitional-duty—Return to Work Plan

The case manager will:
- Monitor the injured worker on transitional-duty to confirm that the RTW date was achieved.
- Identify if there are problems with the transitional-duty job.
- Provide feedback to medical providers to facilitate functional progression of the transitional-duty job and work hours.
- Maintain contact with the injured worker, adjuster, and employer on a monthly basis at minimum.
- Document return to work on transitional-duty and progression toward full duty.
- Communicate to the adjuster regarding the transitional-duty status of the injured worker with timely attention to medical changes that may affect indemnity payments.
- Anticipate progression to full duty, full hours, and pre-injury work status within three months of the referral. The adjuster and employer should be contacted if the injured worker progresses to maximum medical improvement (MMI) while on transitional-duty or sustains a permanent work status or maximum medical improvement.

Chapter 6
DOCUMENTING CASE MANAGEMENT SERVICES

Case managers typically are required to acknowledge receipt from a referral source within twenty-four hours of the referral. Written documentation should be sent to the referral source, typically the claims adjuster. The case manager works with a team of professionals with the main focus of contact being the injured worker, which is more a client-focused approach to providing care. For many years health care has focused on the physician as knowing what is best for the client, today the focus has change to allow the client's insight into decisions on their health care. Use of medical protocols and treatment plans are not enough to achieve positive outcomes, incorporating an injured worker's input into his or her care produces the best case outcome.

Most states identify the parties to the claim as the employer, claims adjuster, injured worker, and medical provider. The case manager is the advocate for the injured worker to assist with his or her medical management and to ensure a safe and timely return to the workforce by the use of proactive initiatives that require communicating with all parties.

The case manager is expected to contact the injured worker or his or her representative; the medical provider and employer should be contacted within two days post referral. All initial contacts should be completed within forty-eight hours followed by documentation in the injured worker's file record. The initial written report may be submitted within thirty days based on the referral, unless the assignment is for a catastrophic case. The case manager is required to notify the claims adjuster if contact failure of any party is experienced, and if a change in the injured worker's medical or work status is determined.

The case manager should use the medical provider's treatment recommendations in conjunction with a workers' compensation evidence-based medical disability treatment guideline in establishing return-to-work criteria. A widely used medical disability treatment guideline resource is offered by the Official Disability Guidelines (ODG), and can be found at www.odg.com.

All documentation should be objective, factual, and accurate, and should include the following written information into a case activity action plan:

- Completion of a medical history and psychosocial assessment form
- Assessment of current work status
- Short- and long-term action plan
- Medical disability guidelines and changes when appropriate
- Compliance with state regulatory guidelines
- Cost savings to demonstrate the value of case management interventions

Establishing Communication with the Treating Medical Provider

Establishing a professional relationship with the treating medical provider is a key role of the case manager. A letter of introduction to the treating medical provider should be followed with a phone call to set the stage for future and ongoing collaborative communication on the injured worker's case.

The case manager should be aware that not all medical providers will view the case manager as the injured worker's advocate. Some medical providers may view the case manager as an insurance advocate, only present to obstruct or deny medical care. These medical providers may believe that the case manager is standing in the way of their treatment plan and may be working against them with the adjuster, looking for ways to deny care.

It is up to the case manager to address this issue if it presents itself by assuring the physician that case manager's advocate for injured workers, not for claim adjusters or insurers.

Case managers, on the other hand, sometimes view medical providers as being detached from caring for the injured worker. Case managers may also feel that medical providers do not show enough interest in treating or in taking the time to correctly diagnose an injured worker's symptoms or that providers use a rubber-stamp approach to workers' compensation injuries in general.

The case manager will be challenged to overcome and dispel any stereotypes applied to healthcare professionals. Conveying a professional mutual respect goes a long way in overcoming stereotypical tendencies. Placing the injured worker's welfare at the heart of all communication should result in successful, collegial relationships. The case manager should promote a positive dialogue with the treating medical provider beginning with the initial contact.

Case managers are to discuss a return to work (RTW) action plan with the treating medical provider (details of the plan should be formulated from employer information and correlated with RTW options in conjunction with professional Medical Disability Guidelines). The case manager should use the treating medical provider's treatment recommendations in conjunction with workers' compensation evidence-based medical guidelines in establishing the return to work criteria. Case managers should obtain medical and RTW status during each physician office encounter.

Case managers should attend ongoing meetings to consult with the injured worker's medical provider to exchange work-related information; to discuss medical treatment expectations; and transitional-duty alternatives. Medical consultation ensures that the case manager will obtain current medical and work related information to update the injured worker's action plan.

The case manager should contact the treating medical provider after receiving the initial referral to:
- Schedule the initial medical provider conference
- Provide RTW options received from the injured worker's employer
- Develop an action plan based on RTW objectives
- Establish future office visits and case conferences

Case Manager Responsibility in Return to Work

The case manager is responsible for ensuring that the appropriate medical release has been obtained from the treating medical provider. The case manager should receive a copy of the injured worker's job description from the employer to analyze it in determining its appropriateness in returning the injured worker to the workplace. The job description outlines the tasks and physical demands of the job, which should be referenced before determining the appropriate transitional-duty job.

Medical clearance should be obtained from the medical provider before the injured worker is ready to return to work. Based on the state of claim adjudication; the case manager, claims adjuster, or medical provider has the responsibility to inform the employer of the injured worker's identified work restrictions and RTW status. The employer is responsible for developing a list of transitional-duty jobs based on the physical capabilities or restrictions identified by the medical provider. The case manager is responsible for reviewing and recommending the transitional-duty job description prior to submitting it to the medical provider for approval.

An RTW plan requires obtaining the following information:
- The restrictions and physical capabilities as identified by the medical provider.
- The transitional-duty RTW date and work hours.
- The work schedule and full-duty progression plan.
- The name of the manager responsible for monitoring the injured worker while on transitional-duty.
- An RTW medical approval. The employer is responsible for developing the RTW plan, reviewing it with the case manager, and making the job offer to the injured worker.
- If the injured worker is terminated, the file should be recommended for vocational rehabilitation to develop a labor market survey to research other potential jobs.

Monitoring Transitional-Duty—Return to Work Plan

The case manager will:
- Monitor the injured worker on transitional-duty to confirm the RTW date was achieved.
- Identify if there are problems with the transitional-duty job.
- Provide feedback to medical providers to facilitate functional progression of the transitional-duty job and work hours.
- Maintain contact with the injured worker, adjuster, and employer on a monthly basis at minimum.
- Document return to work on transitional-duty and progression toward full duty.
- Alert the adjuster about the transitional-duty status of the injured worker, giving timely attention to changes that affect indemnity payments.
- Monitor the injured worker's progress to full duty and pre-injury physical status during the first ninety days of referral.
- Contact the adjuster and employer if the injured worker progresses to maximum medical improvement (MMI) while on transitional-duty or sustains a permanent work status.

- Facilitate a functional capacity evaluation or work-conditioning program to establish work capacity if the employer cannot accommodate an injured worker's ability to RTW. Both assessment options may be used to evaluate the injured worker's functional ability. Work conditioning programs serve to recondition the injured worker for return to work, in instances when the employer is unable to accommodate a transitional job placement.

Referral for Work-Conditioning Programs

Referral to a work-conditioning program is provided when an injured worker cannot be successfully returned to work after injury and recovery. The medical provider may decide to use an authorized physical therapy facility to provide a work-conditioning program for the injured worker whose employer does not have a transitional-duty RTW program. There are several criteria for referral, such as:

- meeting a specific job goal of lifting a certain pound limit as listed in the job description;
- injured worker must have a desire to return to work;
- the medical provider must identify specific neuromuscular skeletal deficits that can be reversed by therapy and;
- the medical injury period must be achieved prior to referral for a work-conditioning program to be effective.

If a work-conditioning program is not a viable option, a vocational rehabilitation referral may be another option to returning the injured worker to suitable employment. If suitable employment is reasonably likely to be available, attempts should be made to place the injured worker in the general labor market. Other choices may be to place the injured worker in a retraining employment program to acquire new job skills.

Medical Disability Timeframes

Medical disability guidelines provide a minimum and a maximum time for recovery by use of five US Division of Labor job classifications. A treatment duration criteria should be used throughout the continuum of case management services. At a minimum, projected time frames should be established by the treating physician to achieve an injured worker's return to work. Medical return to work treatment guidelines are to be used as a resource reference by case managers in their discussions with medical providers. The injured worker's disability duration and time off work should ultimately be determined by the treating medical provider, even though the case manager may offer an opinion.

Case Manager Case Load

The standard caseload for case managers may range from twenty to twenty-five cases at any given time. The caseload is based on the complexity and acuity of the cases and can be adjusted as acuity levels change. For example, it would not be unusual for a caseload to fluctuate to thirty cases that are less active, perhaps primarily requiring monitoring, until minor medical issues are resolved. Such cases typically are those in which the injured worker has returned to work but is being monitored to ensure that the return to work is safe and will not cause a re-injury or relapse to an out-of-work status.

Some injured workers remain out of work for periods of time, sometimes exceeding six months, without the possibility of any RTW option, which typically indicates a severe injury or a need for continued intense medical services. Such patients require more intense case management services and represent most of the case manager's caseload.

An injured worker's noncompliance also should be considered when evaluating case load. The case manager must evaluate each case to determine if the obstacle to case closure is related to noncompliance that may present as missed treatment appointments and may impact the rate of recovery. Both factors will impact the case manager's case load.

Billing for Case Management Services

Case managers are expected to invoice for actual time spent on each claim activity in increments of one-tenth of an hour by rounding up time to the nearest one-tenth of an hour. Case managers should invoice for wait and travel time as non-professional time. All expenses incurred specific to the file such as phone charges, parking, tolls, and charges related to physician conferences are billable at actual costs.

Time Conversion Calculator

Case managers may use this time conversion table to expense for their actual time used in conducting case management activities. For example, a phone call that lasts six minutes may be invoiced as 0.1 of professional case manager's time (see Table 1). In another example, reviewing a medical record may require thirty minutes of actual time, so the case manager may invoice 0.5 of professional time for conducting this activity.

Table 1: Time Conversion Calculator

Time Spent (in Minutes)	Billable Rate (Fraction of an Hour)
06	0.1
12	0.2
18	0.3
24	0.4
30	0.5
36	0.6
42	0.7
48	0.8
54	0.9
60	1.0

Service Code Descriptions and Fee Schedule Guidelines

Service code descriptions and fee schedules provide a comprehensive guide as to what constitutes usual, customary, and reasonable reimbursement for case management services. Fees that are in excess of this fee schedule may be justified by providing documentation of medically necessary services. (See Appendix B, Service Code Descriptions.)

Example: Description of Invoicing using the Fee Schedule Codes

Injured Worker	John Doe			File #		000-9876	
Date	Activity	Service Code	Prof	Expense	Travel/Wait	Miles	Non-Billable
8/3/00	Travel to MD office	706		3.00	2.0	112	
8/3/00	Meet with MD & IW	208	0.5				
8/3/00	Letter to confirm appt	301	0.3				
8/3/00	Visit XYZ Physical Therapy Facility	212	1.0				
8/12/00	TC IW- counseling	506	0.5				
8/22/00	Coordinate IW medical appt	502	0.5				
8/22/00	Assess/Analysis medical record	500	0.5				
8/30/00	Discharge planning	507	1.0				
9/9/00	Coordinate transportation	406	0.5				
9/9/00	Letter to confirm transportation	301	0.3				
9/20/00	Monitor medical services	512	1.0				
9/26/00	Obtain copies of medical records	513	0.5				
9/26/00	Coordinate medical appt	502	0.5				
9/26/00	Reviewed medical documents	515	0.5				
9/27/00	Prepared Action Plan	413	1.5				
9/27/00	Coordinate medical equipment	503	1.0				
9/28/00	Interim Report	414	0.5				
9/28/00	Researched medication	516	0.5				
9/28/00	Telephone call to adjuster	208	0				N/C

Evaluating the Need for Case Closure

In general, a case is ready for closure when an injured worker is released from medical care or has successfully returned to work. Not all cases reach the desired outcome of successful RTW, however. There are times when getting a release to return to work from the treating medical provider is the best available outcome because some injured workers and their employers are opposed to the RTW option. Case managers at the very least should close their files when case management activities can no longer positively impact the outcome of the case. A standard practice is to close the file when the injured worker is released from all medical care by the treating medical provider and has reached maximum medical improvement.

Case managers should maintain ongoing communication with the adjuster by providing them with any changes in medical and psychosocial information that may affect the outcome of the case. A case closure report should be submitted to the adjuster based on the referral information, state regulatory guidelines, or the injured worker, attorney, or adjuster's verbal or written authorization to close the case. In some states, case managers who are employed by a managed care organization or third-party administrator are allowed to remain on a case, even without authorization from the attorney or injured worker. Some states consider the employed case manager a party to the file as the adjuster is viewed in claim handling. For this reason, some states will allow case manager involvement even if the attorney refuses injured worker contact because there is a documented cost savings on claims when case managers are used to manage care.

Cost Containment

Case management is the best cost-containment resource available in handling workers' compensation files. Case managers can reduce claim costs by getting the injured worker to the appropriate medical provider and by expediting tests and procedures in a timely manner, which results in preventing unnecessary delays or complications in care. Case managers are skilled in using medical treatment guideline data to track and trend estimated recovery times that trigger a second opinion or an independent medical evaluation, which are accepted in expediting case progression to closure if no objective treatment guidelines are identified. Companies that are informed and want to reduce claim costs make use of case management in their cost saving plans. Case managers are medical professionals who can equally assist the injured worker, adjuster, and employer in consulting on healthcare issues.

Cost Savings

The benefit of case management interventions have been identified over several decades. These interventions date back to World War II when case managers coordinated care for wounded soldiers. The practice of facilitating required medical services and coordinating care is the paramount role and function of the case manager, which leads to major cost savings on each claim served. In workers' compensation, it is expected that case managers will complete a cost savings report on each closed case. Medical savings may be achieved by managing the costs related to duplication of services for medications, diagnostic tests, therapy sessions, surgeries, or other treatments that may be ordered by multiple physicians throughout the continuum of care. Case managers are skilled in expediting care which is shown to aide in recovery by getting the injured worker the optimal care when needed.

Indemnity cost savings may be realized when the case manager facilitates an early RTW, full-duty or a transitional- duty return to work job is achieved.

Prescription Medication Costs and Independent Medical Examinations

The last two areas to cover are prescription medication cost and independent medical examinations (IME) to demonstrate the value added by case managers coordinating these services. To improve on managed care, it is important for the case manager to ensure that the injured worker does not experience a fatal or life-threatening drug interaction. This is done by reviewing all medication utilization by conducting monthly interviews with the injured worker and by educating the injured worker on medication compliance and management.

Case managers may achieve cost savings through monitoring and coordinating the injured worker's medication compliance by using a certified pharmacy benefit plan, negotiated discounts, or using generic medication substitutions whenever indicated. Cost savings may also be achieved by using an employer's Preferred Provider Organization (PPO), or mail order pharmacy vendor or by not allowing an injured worker to purchase their own medications at higher costs. Another cost savings benefit case managers offer is medication management which reduces the incidents of drug interaction and/or drug duplication, which prevents life threatening complication or death.

Independent medical evaluations (IMEs) have been used by insurance carriers and attorneys alike in attempt to clarify complex medical diagnosis or in determining an injured worker's physical limitations. In addition, some IME requests are based on questionable impairment rating determinations and are also used is in determining the need for surgical intervention. Case managers play a critical role in that many carriers rely on them to make the IME referral. IME physicians are selected based on their ability to render an independent opinion, as well as on their specialty area of practice. For these reasons, the case manager should remain ethical in the selection choice of the IME physician and become knowledgeable of the selection process to guarantee an unbiased decision in advocating for the rights of their client. The case manager should keep in mind that advocating for a return to work status for the injured worker is medically appropriate and within the scope of a good ethical practice, because the IME physician's decision is based on medical evidence.

Report Format

The case manager should provide written or verbal updates throughout the case assignment until the claim is closed for case management services. A claim may be closed for case management, but may continue to remain open until the claim adjuster is able to reach a claim settlement. With most referred assignments, the case manager is expected to complete an initial report within forty-eight hours of the initial injured worker's interview. An initial report, a monthly medical status interim report and a final closure report, are all required written documents to be submitted to the adjuster, and are also considered requirements until conclusion of the case assignment. Depending on state requirements, the attorneys also may request a copy of the monthly written report. The case manager should be aware that the referring agency may restrict or limit the case manager's ability to forward documents to certain parties to the claim based on case litigation; which may include all verbal and written material. Therefore, parties to the claim to whom communication is privileged should establish communication standards at the time of case manager referral.

Case managers will typically be responsible for completing and submitting one report per month, or sooner, as requested in the referral assignment or in circumstances where a change in medical condition occurs. The type of report a case manager completes depends on the specific account referral instructions, which may state the referral is for a medical task, and/or full or catastrophic case manager assignment. The report types are usually an initial, meaning first; an interim, meaning any reporting that occurs between the initial and final report, which is also referred to as a closure report. A Task Report may only require one report. The report types are usually initial—meaning first—and interim, meaning any reporting that occurs between the initial and final report, which is also referred to as a closure report. There are no minimum or maximum reports that may be submitted on a single case. The number of completed reports is dependent on the injured worker's acuity level during the course of the case management assignment.

Each report should include goals and objectives necessary to achieve a specific task in an assigned time frame. The objectives should be stated in measurable terms and should be related to the established goal. The reports should include documentation from in-person interviews with the injured worker and medical provider. The development of the report will include comments related to cost containment, quality of care, and description of services provided during each reporting period. In addition, the case manager should include the date the report was submitted to the claims adjuster, injured worker and his/her attorney of representation.

All reports should begin with the injured worker's name, claim number, and date of the report. The report should end with the case manager's name, signature, credentials, title, phone number, and e-mail address. All reports should have appropriate objective documentation. Elements of the report may include SOAP documentation: subjective comments, objective findings, assessments, and an action plan. Subjective comments should be recorded during each visit, and any medical changes should be noted. Objective findings should include any clinical conditions, treatments, and description of all treatment progress. Assessments should include objective findings related to goals. Action plans should be recorded on a regular basis, with changes made as necessary toward achieving goals.

Task Reports:
- Task assignments can be a one-time assignment or may comprise several limited assignments based on the specific referral instructions.

- A task report should include an anticipated RTW date including a list of the injured worker's physical work restrictions
- The body of the report must include all care coordination activities relevant to the case management assignment.
- The action plan must include medical provider contact information, particularly the name of the provider, specialty, address, phone number, and date and time of subsequent appointments.
- Task assignments typically are closed after the goal is met, which could be a single activity or may require additional activities before closure is achieved.

Initial Report Format

An initial report is completed by the case manager typically within thirty days postdate of referral, unless the case assignment is requested for a catastrophic case. The type of report format used is dependent on the specific case manager referral assignment.

The initial report should contain:
- Injured worker history, including a description of injury or illness and subsequent treatment.
- Treating diagnosis and prognosis, including an explanation of the medical status and probability for recovery.
- Specific treatment site, including notes as to whether the injured worker's symptoms are related to the injury and diagnosis.
- Case manager assessment, including an explanation of the appropriateness of the medical care based on the injured worker's diagnosis and symptoms and how the medical provider addressed the injured worker's symptoms and physical limitations in the medical treatment plan. The assessment also should address the effects of any pre-existing medical and/or surgical conditions.
- Maximum medical improvement (MMI) options such as a functional capacity evaluation (FCE) or work-conditioning program used to meet the injured worker's maximum medical improvement needs.
- Medical provider appointments, including all medical appointments listing the specialist and contact information.

- Work status, including all physical restrictions and limitations, as well as a potential RTW date that matches the job demands to the injured worker's current functional abilities.
- Action plans listing short- and long-term goals to assist in determining if any medical or non-medical issues may affect positive outcomes.

Interim Report Format

Interim reports are submitted to the adjuster and used to monitor the injured worker's medical progress until the case is closed for case management. SOAP note format may be used. Specific objective detail must be given to support the billing activity as documented. The interim report should address:

- Summary of current medical status, secondary conditions affecting recovery, treatment, prognosis since the previous medical examination.
- Work status, including an explanation as to whether the injured worker is capable of returning to work at any work level.
- Medical provider appointment information, including notes as to whether the injured worker is receiving ongoing medical care that indicates progression toward recovery.
- Action plans listing short- and long-term goals to assist in determining if any medical or non-medical issues are affecting positive outcomes.
- Indicate whether the injured worker will benefit from further case manager involvement on the case.

Closure Report Format

- A case manager will typically close a case when a medical provider releases the injured worker to MMI and full-work duty. The case manager may decide to monitor the injured worker for one month post medical provider discharge to ensure that the injured worker is successful in RTW transition. The reason for case closure should be listed in the closure report which is submitted to the adjuster or other parties listed on the initial referral assignment.
- Medical status, including an explanation as to the disposition of the injured worker's medical status resulting in file closure.

- Work status, including an explanation of any physical restrictions or functional limitations at the time of medical discharge. Document when the injured worker was able to return to work.
- Goals achieved; including documentation as to which action plan items were achieved, and how to move the case toward a successful outcome.
- Cost-saving reports should be completed on all case types to capture the cost benefit achieved by the case manager.

Measures to Ensure Case Management Quality

On a monthly basis, a minimum of 10 percent of all files, at a minimum, should be reviewed for case manager compliance with key performance elements. The key performance elements should include the case manager compliance in meeting the state or employer performance standards. These elements are reviewed and rated in terms of compliance based on the case management employer or state standards. Each element is given an actual point value which is compared to the maximum point value of 100 percent. These monthly profiles can be utilized in conjunction with monthly production activity reports to identify specific outcome data, or serve to improve case manager performance standards. Ten percent of the case manager's completed work product is reviewed by the employer's designee on a monthly basis for tracking and trending of outcomes. Evaluation standards are based on:

- Compliance with case management, state, and employer standards of practice
- Four-point contact included documentation with: injured worker, employer, adjuster, and medical provider
- Adherence to thirty day reporting timelines
- Compliance with referral reporting guidelines
- Monthly case load production levels
- Accuracy of invoicing case manager activity
- Accuracy of report content documentation
- Care coordination implementation action plan
- Evaluation of outcomes

CASE MANAGER WORK SHEET

Case Manager receives referral from referral source.

↓

Case manager makes initial contact with adjuster to discuss account instructions.

↓

Case Manager establishes four point communication within 48 hours of referral and documents this communication within the file record.
- Contact Adjuster: Discuss injury, account instructions, or claim issues
- Contact Employer: Discuss mechanism of injury, request job description, transitional duty.
- Contact IW: Explain CM role, obtain verbal consent to coordinate care, obtain IW's assessment of their medical status.
- Contact Medical Provider: Determine treatment plan, provide IW's job description, discuss RTW options..
- Contact Attorney: Obtain consent to interact with client on all files where IW is represented.

↓

Establishes a case management action plan that provides for short-term and long-term goals, based on the type of referral (Task, Full, CAT, TCM). Re-evaluations case progress through ongoing collaboration with all parties until case closure.

↓

- Maintain continuous telephonic follow-up based on changes in IWs condition.
- Develop CM Action Plan based on medical treatment guidelines.
- Coordinate care to appropriate providers
- Facilitate RTW action plan with employer coordination.
- Consult with medical provider/IW and revise CM Action Plan as needed..

↓

Case Manager Reporting
- Updates adjuster on significant changes
- Revises CM action plan as needed.
- Written reports every 30 days.

↓

File Closure
- IW reaches MMI
- Successful RTW full duty
- Permanent restrictions
- Referral source request file closure.

Chapter 1-6 Summary

Case Managers can maximize the employer workers' compensation dollar by using case management strategies in controlling medical costs.

Case managers can assist in cost containment by implementing best practice strategies and by becoming a resource liaison in the workers' compensation industry. Case managers:

1. Identify the role managed care plays in workers' compensation injuries. State law requires that the injured worker is afforded access to medical care. This access may be in the form of a panel of physicians, a state approved managed care organization, or an employer agreement of a medical provider selection. In some states, unauthorized medical treatment will not be covered.
2. Identify inefficiencies in the workers' compensation system and apply solutions to overcoming them. An issue that frequently arises is who is the authorized treating physician that all medical care should be directed through?
3. Identify if a causal relation exists between the injury and the incident. Workers' compensation laws cover only those injuries or industrial conditions that are related to on-the-job incidents.
4. Identify the medical signs and symptoms of the injury or illness. The injured worker's medical conditions should be addressed and reimbursed within the workers' compensation system. In addition, private health insurance will not cover a workers' compensation injury.
5. Identify what skills the injured worker possesses in order to develop a transitional duty job and determine readiness for return to work. Return to work initiatives should be implemented only with approval (signed statement) from the authorized treating medical provider.
6. Identify and establish a working relationship with medical providers. A medical provider makes treatment decisions based on development of a professional relationship and factual information provided by the case manager.

7. Maintain open, ongoing communication with all parties of the claim. The case manager must remain a neutral liaison who communicates with all parties to the claim as advocate for the injured worker.
8. Identify unresolved medical symptoms and request appropriate medical referrals. In situations where the case manager observes that the injured worker has not achieved an appreciable recovery, a recommendation should be made for an independent medical evaluation in the best interest of the injured worker.
9. Coordinate care and follow-up until the injured worker reaches maximum medical care. Maximum medical improvement is determined by the authorized treating physician and is not time limited.
10. Participate in consultation with the injured worker and medical provider at routine office appointments. The case manager should facilitate an open dialogue to ensure the injured worker understands their diagnosis, treatment plan, and prognosis for return to work. In addition, reviews the injured worker's symptoms and test results to revise action plans.
11. Discuss return to work issues with the injured worker and medical provider. If the injured worker is unable to return to work, he or she should be referred for a functional capacity test and/or for vocational rehabilitation services to expedite a return to work unless the injury is catastrophic.
12. Review the medical provider's treatment plan and prognosis for full recovery. A medical provider treatment plan should indicate a pattern that progresses the injured worker toward maximum recovery and optimal function.
13. Explore the issue of secondary gain and how it affects recovery and return to work. Patient advocacy includes patient compliance with medical care. If the injured worker is non-compliant with medical care, it is the case manager's responsibility to explore and discuss this issue with the injured worker and medical provider.

Questions the case manager can ask to address lost time days?
- Are out of work days based on objective medical facts?
- Are there out of work days that some capacity of work could be productive?

Case managers don't accept out of work excuses:
- Medical provider did not provide a return to work release. Why?
- Requested medical records were not provided. Why?
- Employer will not provide a transitional duty job. Why?
- Injured worker refuses to return to work. Why?

Case managers must define the problem before listing steps to resolution:
- What obstacles are preventing the injured worker from returning to work?
- Would the injured worker be work ready if he owned the company?

The case manager's action plan includes:
- Assertive case intervention
- Teamwork communication
- Addressing medically appropriate care
- Coordinating, monitoring, and evaluating medical care
- Assessing for a transitional duty job
- Reviewing job site safety for return to work

Positive outcomes through case management strategies:
- Ensure the injured worker receives quality medical care
- Reduce injuries by implementing safety protocols and awareness
- Early case management interventions to reduce the overall claim costs
- Care coordination of cases tend to close cases earlier
- Implementation of a return to work plan keeps the injured worker engaged and connected to the work place
- Manage obstacles by collaborating with parties to the claim; the injured worker, the employer, the medical provider, the adjuster

Case managers can address obstacles in returning an injured worker to work by:
- Being the link between the injured worker and the employer
- Monitoring and implementing changes until the case is closed

- Communicating medical information to the employer to plan for the injured worker's absence from the work plan
- Assisting the employer in developing a transitional duty job
- Communicating the importance of keeping the injured worker productive
- Educating the employer on the importance of creating a safe work place to reduce lost time claims

Employers can maximize their workers' compensation dollar by implementing case management strategies!

Chapter 7
STATE-BY-STATE WORKERS' COMPENSATION CASE MANAGEMENT REGULATIONS

Purpose

The information and material contained in this section is intended to be general information regarding rules and regulations on workers' compensation case management that cover the fifty states in the continental US, as well as the District of Columbia. It is not intended to be used as a substitute for the employer or carrier policies and procedures, or legal counsel or advice on specific case management practice.

This guide was developed to serve as a quick reference specifically for case managers who work in the field of workers' compensation field. The state case management rules and regulations cited here were researched and certain topics were adapted from each state workers' compensation website. Topics and information included in this guide were specifically chosen with the sole intent to provide answers to the most frequently asked questions that effect everyday case manager activities.

Prior to the existence of this reference guide, there was no quick comprehensive guide to access the state information needed by most workers' compensation case managers who practice across state lines. This guide intends to reduce the time and stress spent having to conduct individual state website searches. It is not intended as legal or medical advice to case managers. Readers and users of this guide are encouraged to seek professional legal advice on how your state's workers' compensation statutes apply to your independent case management practice.

General Information

As you are aware, workers' compensation insurance is a no-fault insurance coverage provided by employers for their employees; coverage is mandated at both the state and federal levels. The workers' compensation insurance system offers coverage for injured workers, while protecting the employers from personal lawsuits by limiting settlement remedies to state legislated statues. The principles of the workers' compensation laws are very similar in each state, but each state has adapted different benefit packages that effect their indemnity payment benefits and medical coverage.

In addition to the differences in state workers' compensation benefit packages, case manager coverage for medical case management services or vocational rehabilitation services may be included in some states, but may be excluded in others. There are some states that will assign the responsibility to cover case management services to insurance carriers or employers in determining the need for these services. In general, insurance carriers and employers tend to support the use of case managers in claims handling as a positive adjunct measure to achieving successful outcomes in claims management.

The Workers Compensation Insurance Industry has led in the field of health care delivery by offering case management services as a benefit to improving healthcare delivery and cost containment as part of the claims management package in most states. Some states have led by legislating case manager qualification and credentialing practice standards. Some states have regulations for managed care organizations, while others resort to utilization review or bill review to solve some of their workers' compensation cost containment issues. Many states are also looking at becoming more innovative by using medical disability treatment guidelines to control claim costs. There are several companies that market evidenced-based treatment guidelines that have gained recognition and approval from the Agency for Health Care Research and Quality (AHRQ).

State-by-State Cost Containment

The field of case management has been around for over more than thirty years, and there will continue to be a need as healthcare costs continues to escalate. The workers' compensation medical client mix continues to be a challenging field. Several factors contribute to this, such as:

- more elderly individuals remain in the workforce,
- more employees who have other chronic medical conditions that impact an on-the-job injury,
- more catastrophic injuries with increasing survival rates, and
- more uninsured workers today than ever before, who may use the state workers' compensation benefit system for non-related care.

Case managers are aware that workers compensation insurance coverage can only be used for an on-the-job injury and will locate other resources for injured workers who are not covered under other medical insurance plans.

Several states use of cost containment can be seen is in establishing state fee payment schedules by, use of managed care organizations, preferred provider organizations, physician panels, utilization review, medical treatment guidelines, standardized impairment ratings; and bill review. Most states are using cost containment measures to reduce spending on claim costs that are determined as medically un-necessary services. For example, use of medical disability treatment guidelines are researched evidence-based medicine and are used by more state systems and managed care organizations in reducing the duration and frequency of injuries. The AHRQ highlights the importance of using scientific evidence based medical treatment guidelines as providing a standardized medical care plan which offers a cost savings benefit. Some states have adapted their own medical treatment guidelines, which may not be evidence-based or offer medical facts supported by peer review research. In states that adopted medical treatment guidelines instead of using managed care organizations, or physician panels, are tracking the guideline's effectiveness in controlling cost. Collecting and trending data will provide a mechanism for states to develop a comprehensive workers' compensation system model for general usage.

Many states have resorted to use of Managed Care Organizations (MCOs) in their efforts to control cost. Managed care refers to assessing, coordinating and delivering health care services as the need is identified by employers, self-insurers, insurance carriers and injured workers or clients.

The following are types of managed care organizations (MCOs) that will be reference throughout this text. References will be made to state/employer arranged MCOs and their use and function in providing services to injured workers while remaining at the center in controlling state medical cost. MCOs usually offer a fixed fee for a package of multiple services they administer. Some states may use a mixture of these services as a cost containment effort.

- Managed Care Organizations (MCOs) usually own a network of medical care services such as physician networks, hospitals and physical therapy services. MCOs can control cost by using a pool of negotiated services and fixed fees, by establishing policies that govern access, and by eliminating fragmentation of service delivery.

- Health Maintenance Organizations (HMOs) use an ambulatory staff-model practice for administering medical care, which usually provides a full range of services such as laboratory, x-ray, and ancillary services. HMOs may contract with hospitals for in-patient services for their beneficiaries.

- Preferred Provider Organizations (PPOs) cover beneficiaries from selected participating employers/insurers. Medical providers are required to adhere to utilization review procedures per their PPO plan. Medical providers are typically paid at a discounted rate. Beneficiaries have the option under certain circumstances to use medical providers that are not in the PPO network, but usually at a higher fee rate.

Managed care organizations can achieve the goal to lowering costs for medical care through negotiated rates, as well as improving efficiency of service delivery by managing care from the onset of a claim until the claim closes. By providing the appropriate medical care from the onset of an injury, the MCO can reduce medical complications and the need for expensive interventions by specialists or in-patient hospital care. Another area where MCO's manage care is through use of case managers and vocational rehabilitation specialists.

Case managers may be employed by a state certified MCO, and/or may work with the MCO's contracted employer. Whichever service provider arrangement is used, case managers and rehabilitation professionals are required to comply with the state practice standards governing their profession. Typically states will require the following credentials for professionals practicing worker's compensation case management: CCM, CRRN, CHON, COHN-S, LPC, CEAVES, CDMS, or CRC. The MCO is required to file names and credentials with the worker's compensation board of those practicing case management wherever a state mandate exist. In addition, the MCO must attest that all of their case managers have the appropriate credentials.

Case managers working in the rehabilitation service area work under the titles of rehabilitation consultant or counselor. Many states endorse rehabilitation services rather than medical case management par se because these services focus merely on returning the injured worker back to work rather than focusing on coordination of medical care. RTW efforts target reducing indemnity payments which is beneficial in reducing the out of work cost. What is the difference between a rehabilitation consultant and a vocational rehabilitation counselor?

1. A rehabilitation consultant is typically a professional individual employed outside of the employer/insurer/TPA who is hired by the adjuster to provide guidance on the injured worker's medical and/or rehabilitation needs.

2. Vocational rehabilitation counselor (VCR) is a professional who works closely with clients that are coping with physical injuries, mental illness, psychological disorders, or substance abuse issues. VRCs interact with these clients and their families, as well as physicians, speech therapists, physical therapists, and psychologists.

3. Vocational rehabilitation services include all services necessary to assist a client with a limiting disability to secure, retain, or regain employment that is consistent with the client's abilities, capabilities, interests, and informed choice.

A Guide to Successful Worker's Compensation

By virtue of thirty-nine states having legislated some form of worker's compensation managed care, an understanding is demonstrated of the added cost savings benefit of providing case management services. As states continue to track and trend the benefits of offering case management services, the resultant research will continue to validate the value that case managers add to healthcare delivery. It is of the utmost importance that all parties in the workers' compensation industry understand the added value the case manager brings to each case is their ability to coordinate medical care and ensure the delivery of quality health care is provided based on the level of care as needed. This type of client-centered case manager advocacy approach to managing health care improves client satisfaction, aids in controlling claim cost by not delaying care, and expedites case closure by diminishing medical complications through early interventions that target medical recovery.

Other areas aside from case manager services where states use cost containment initiatives can be seen is in establishing state fee payment schedules, by use of managed care organizations, preferred provider organizations, physician panels, utilization review, medical treatment guidelines, standardized impairment ratings, and bill review. Most states are using these methods to reduce unnecessary spending on claim related costs that are seen as not necessary to medical recovery or determined to be outside customary charges in a specific location. For example, the Official Disability Guidelines (ODG) has been in use since 1996. It is viewed as evidence-based medicine and is being used by more state systems and managed care organizations to reduce the duration and frequency a determined diagnosed condition is eligible for care. The AHRQ highlights the use of scientific evidence based medical treatment guidelines as providing a standardized care plan which offers a cost savings benefit. Many states are adapting their own medical treatment guidelines, which may not be evidence-based or offer medical facts supported by peer review research. In situations where we see states that are using medical treatment guidelines instead of managed care organizations or physician panels as a cost control measure, the state guidelines should be enforced and tracked consistently to determine their effectiveness in controlling cost. This provides a way to establish a state model for comprehensive workers' compensation system usage. The goal of tracking successful case management outcomes would be best served by using the results of this study to create a best practice state medical treatment guideline to be a model for each state's practice.

STATE WORKERS' COMPENSATION CASE MANAGEMENT REGULATIONS

ALABAMA	63
ALASKA	65
ARIZONA	67
ARKANSAS	69
CALIFORNIA	72
COLORADO	75
CONNECTICUT	78
DELAWARE	81
DISTRICT OF COLUMBIA	84
FLORIDA	86
GEORGIA	88
HAWAII	91
IDAHO	94
ILLINOIS	97
INDIANA	100
IOWA	103
KANSAS	105
KENTUCKY	108
LOUISIANA	110
MAINE	113
MARYLAND	1145
MASSACHUSETTS	117
MICHIGAN	120
MINNESOTA	123
MISSISSIPPI	126
MISSOURI	128
MONTANA	131
NEBRASKA	134
NEVADA	137
NEW HAMPSHIRE	140
NEW JERSEY	143
NEW MEXICO	145

NEW YORK	148
NORTH CAROLINA	151
NORTH DAKOTA	155
OHIO	159
OKLAHOMA	163
OREGON	166
PENNSYLVANIA	168
RHODE ISLAND	171
SOUTH CAROLINA	173
SOUTH DAKOTA	175
TENNESSEE	178
TEXAS	180
UTAH	183
VERMONT	185
VIRGINIA	187
WASHINGTON	189
WEST VIRGINIA	191
WISCONSIN	193
WYOMING	195

ALABAMA

Alabama Department of Industrial Relations
649 Monroe Street
Montgomery, Alabama 36131
Telephone: 1-800-528-5166 (toll free) or (334) 242-2868

State Website: dir.alabama.gov/wc

State Rules and Regulations for Case Management

Professionals performing medical case management must comply with the state standards adopted by the National Association of Rehabilitation Professionals in the Private Sector (NARPPS). Alabama has identified professional performance criteria for medical case management; which pertains to workers' compensation cases or other nationally recognized medical case management.

Medical case management determination is stated to be the responsibility of the employer, unless delegated to another entity. Case management services may be performed in conjunction with utilization management.

The state defines the overall goal of medical case management as facilitating appropriate health care services. Case management services should be implemented in the most cost-effective manner without compromising quality of care in order to promote optimal outcomes for all parties involved.

Access to Medical Care

The employer's authorized treating physician must be the physician of claim record.

All case management referrals should be pre-approved by the employer or its agent. The employer or its agent should keep the adjuster or insurance carrier informed of any change in the authorized treating physician. The choice of treating physician is limited to the employer. The injured worker is allowed to change physicians by selecting from a list of four employer provided physicians.

When the treating physician recommends elective surgery, the injured worker is subject to the limitations of Alabama's code. The employer is entitled to obtain a second medical opinion from another board certified physician of the same or similar specialty to confirm a need for surgery, but it is not required.

State Fee Schedule Guidelines

The fee schedule is mandatory, unless payment is worked out with the provider or a preferred provider network.

Medical Necessity and Medical Treatment Guidelines

Utilization management is a comprehensive set of integrated components including: pre-certification review, admission review, continued stay review, retrospective review, discharge planning, bill screening, and individual medical case management as required. Utilization management and bill screening may be implemented, but are not required. Only agencies qualified by the department may perform certain functions listed as utilization review management.

Permanent Impairment Rating

The American Medical Association Guides to the Evaluation of Permanent Impairment, Fourth Edition, is the recommended guide used by physicians in determining impairment and/or disability ratings.

ALASKA

Alaska Department of Labor and Workforce Development
Division of Workers' Compensation
1111 W 8th Street, Room 305
Juneau, AK 99801
Telephone: (907) 465-2790
Fax: (907) 465-2797

State Website: labor.state.ak.us/wc

State Rules and Regulations for Case Management

Rehabilitation specialists designated to practice in the state must be a licensed provider and certified by the state of Alaska.

A "certified insurance rehabilitation specialist" means a person currently certified by the Certification of Insurance Rehabilitation Specialists Commission.

Access to Medical Care

The injured worker may choose a licensed doctor to treat their injury (including a licensed medical doctor, surgeon, chiropractor, osteopath, dentist, or optometrist). The injured worker may change the treating doctor once, but must inform the insurer before making the change. If the doctor refers the injured worker to a specialist, the referral will not count as a change of doctors. If the injured worker makes a doctor change, written approval must be obtained from the insurer. If the injured worker changes doctors more than once without the insurer's written approval, the injured worker may be responsible for payment of the doctor's bills.

Second Independent Medical Evaluation (SIME)

When the injured worker's physician and the insurer's physician disagree on the nature or extent of the injury or illness, a party may request an examination by a physician chosen by the Board of Workers Compensation.

State Fee Schedule Guidelines

The state has a mandatory fee schedule.

Medical Necessity and Medical Treatment Guidelines

Utilization review is not mandatory. There are no state related medical treatment guidelines.

The state does define payment for repeated treatments of the same kind, such as physical therapy or chiropractic care. The insurer usually will not have to pay for outpatient treatment in excess of: three times per week for the first month, two times per week for the second and third months, once a week for the fourth and fifth months, and once a month for the sixth through twelfth months. If the injured worker's physician determines that more treatment is indicated, the physician must submit a written treatment plan within fourteen days of the initial treatment. If a written treatment plan is not sent to the insurer within fourteen days after the first treatment, the insurer may not be required to reimburse the physician for services.

Permanent Impairment Rating

The state takes a position of assumption that the American Medical Association's (AMA) Guides to the Evaluation of Permanent Impairment will be used in addressing an injury. If the board finds the presumption is overcome by clear and convincing evidence, and if the permanent impairment cannot—in the board's opinion—be determined under the AMA guides, then the impairment rating must be based on the Permanent Partial Disability Schedule or the American Academy of Orthopedic Surgeons' (AAOS) *Manual For Evaluating Permanent Physical Impairments*. If a rating under the Permanent Partial Disability Schedule or the AAOS is not of the whole person, the rating must be converted to a whole person rating under the AMA guides.

ARIZONA

Industrial Commission of Arizona (ICA)
800 W. Washington Street
Phoenix, AZ 85007
Telephone: (602) 542-4661

General Website: www.ica.state.az.us

State Rules and Regulations for Case Management

The Arizona Regulation on the Special Fund has discretionary power in providing vocational rehabilitation benefits. While rehabilitation is not mandatory in Arizona, the statutes specify that the Special Fund can provide assistance in this area if requested by the insurance carrier or the injured worker, and if certain criteria are met. The Special Fund promotes and assists in vocational rehabilitation delivery, both on scheduled and unscheduled injuries. Since these are two distinct categories, the Special Fund's participation, policy statements, and costs may vary.

Access to Medical Care

An employer can direct an injured worker to a physician of the employer's choice for a one-time evaluation. After the initial visit, the injured worker may return to that physician or pursue treatment with a physician of his/her choice.

The rule has an exception. While a self-insured injured employee that has complied with requirements—after the initial visit to the employer's designated physician—may report to a physician of his/her choice, employees that are self-insured with contracted medical care are required to use the employer's contracted doctors for all medical care related to the industrial injury.

Once an attending physician is selected, there are three ways to change doctors: the attending physician refers the injured worker to another doctor; the insurance carrier approves a change of doctors; or upon written application from the injured worker the ICA approves a change of doctors.

Additionally, if both the injured worker's doctor and insurance carrier refuse the worker's request to change doctors, the worker may apply to the Industrial Commission for approval to change doctors.

State Fee Schedule Guidelines

The state fee schedule is mandatory.

Medical Necessity and Medical Treatment Guidelines

Utilization review is not mandated. There are no medical treatment guidelines.

Permanent Impairment Rating

There are two kinds of permanent impairments, scheduled and unscheduled. Both types are paid on a monthly basis.

A scheduled injury refers to a specific body part. The Arizona Workers' Compensation Law sets out a schedule indicating the amounts to be paid for these impairments. There is also compensation payable for visible facial scarring and loss of permanent teeth.

An unscheduled injury is the result of a general impairment, a combination of impairments to different body parts injured in one incident, or a history of other permanent impairments. In these cases, the ICA determines what amount of compensation the injured worker is entitled to based on loss of earning capacity.

Many factors are involved in these decisions, such as limitations, education, work experience, etc. In some cases, there is no monetary award, as the injured worker has returned to work earning the same or in excess of the established average monthly wage. These awards take approximately ninety days from the issuance of the notices by the insurance carrier.

ARKANSAS

Arkansas Workers' Compensation Commission
324 Spring Street
Little Rock, AR 72203-0950
Telephone: (800-622-4472 (toll free) or, (501) 682-3930

State Website: www.awcc.state.ar.us

State Rules and Regulations for Case Management

A medical case manager for the purposes of Arkansas' Rule means an individual who provides or supervises the provision of medical case management services under the MCO and who is either:

1) a physician licensed in Arkansas; or
2) a Designated Certified Case Manager (CCM) by the Certification of Insurance Rehabilitation Specialists Commission for Case Manager Certification; or
3) currently licensed as a Registered Nurse (RN); or
4) currently licensed as an Occupational Health Nurse; or
5) Currently licensed as a Licensed Practical Nurse (LPN) and have eighteen months supervised clinical experience and six months acceptable case management experience.

The state defines a medical case manager's role as monitoring, evaluating, and coordinating the delivery of quality, cost-effective medical treatment and other health care services needed by an injured worker. Medical case managers should ensure that the injured or disabled employee is following the prescribed medical care plan, and shall promote an appropriate, prompt return to work. Medical case managers should also facilitate communication between the injured worker, employer, insurance carrier, self-insured, health care provider, managed care plan, and any assigned vocational rehabilitation counselor to achieve stated goals.

Vocational Rehabilitation Services

The injured worker should not be required to enter any program of vocational rehabilitation against his or her consent; no injured worker who refuses to participate in either an offered program of rehabilitation or job placement assistance, should be entitled to permanent partial disability benefits in excess of the percentage of permanent physical impairment established by objective physical findings.

Access to Medical Care

The employer has the right to select the initial primary care physician from among those associated with managed care entities certified by the Commission. The Insurance Commissioner may allow a rate reduction for employers who use their carriers' contracted Managed Care Organizations (MCOs) exclusively.

Employees should initially request a change of physician from the insurance carrier/employer/self-insured employer. Within five business days of the employee's initial request for a change of physician, the insurance carrier/employer/self-insured employer shall notify the employee of its decision to grant or deny the change of physician.

Where the employer has a contract with a managed care organization, certified by the Commission, the injured worker should be allowed to change physicians by petitioning the Commission for a one-time change of physician. The physician must be associated with any managed care entity certified by the Commission or be the regular treating physician of the employee who maintains the employee's medical records and with whom the employee has a bona fide doctor-patient relationship. If the treating physician agrees to refer the injured worker to a physician associated with a managed care organization, that physician must agree to comply with all state rules.

State Fee Schedule Guidelines

The state fee schedule is mandatory. The carrier is required to provide the Medical Cost Containment Division with the name, address, and license number (and a copy of the contract agreement between the carrier and other entity, if applicable) of the entity responsible for conducting the carrier's utilization review program.

Medical Necessity and Medical Treatment Guidelines

The insurance carrier is required to have a utilization review program. The insurance carrier may have another certified entity perform utilization review activities on its behalf. The utilization review program, whether operated by the carrier or an entity on behalf of the carrier, shall be certified by the Arkansas State Board of Health.

Permanent Impairment Rating

Similar to Alaska, The Arkansas Workers' Compensation Commission has adopted the AMA fourth Edition *Guides to the Evaluation of Permanent Impairment* exclusive of any sections which refer to pain and exclusive of straight leg raising tests or range of motion tests when making physical or anatomical impairment ratings to the spine.

CALIFORNIA

California Division of Workers' Compensation
1515 Clay Street, 6th Floor
Oakland, CA 94612-1402
Telephone: (800) 736-7401 (toll free) or (510) 286-7100

State Website: www.dir.ca.gov/DWC

State Rules and Regulations for Case Management

Vocational Return to Work Counselor

The state regulation requires the employer or insurance carrier to notify the injured worker of the availability of rehabilitation services for disabilities that continue for twenty-eight days or more. Notification of available rehabilitation services should be made at the time the injured worker is paid retroactively for the first day of disability (in cases of twenty-eight days of continuing disability or hospitalization), which has previously been uncompensated.

Rehabilitation Counselor

If the treating physician indicates that the injured worker will not be able to return to their usual occupation or job as a result of their injury, the injured worker may be entitled to rehabilitation benefits. A rehabilitation program includes services which are reasonably necessary to return the injured worker to suitable gainful employment.

A rehabilitation counselor will be assigned and the counselor will assist in the preparation of the program, taking into consideration the injury, past working experience, transferable skills, motivation and the labor market. While actively engaged in the rehabilitation program, the injured worker will continue to receive either temporary disability benefits or a rehabilitation maintenance allowance, depending on the date of injury.

Access to Medical Care

Doctors in California's workers' compensation system are required to provide evidence-based medical treatment. That means they must choose treatments scientifically proven to cure or relieve work-related injuries and illnesses. Those treatments are laid out in the Medical Treatment Utilization Schedule (MTUS), which contains a set of guidelines that provide details on: effective treatments for certain injuries, how often the treatment should be given, the extent of the treatment, and length of treatment.

Under California regulations, each Managed Plan Network(MPN) must include a mix of doctors specializing in work-related injuries and doctors with expertise in general areas of medicine. MPNs are required to meet access to care standards for common occupational injuries and work-related illnesses. The regulations also require MPNs to follow all medical treatment guidelines established by the Division of Worker's Compensation (DWC) that allow employees a choice of provider(s) in the network after their first visit. Additionally, MPNs must offer an opportunity for second and third opinions if the injured worker disagrees with the diagnosis or treatment offered by the treating physician. If a disagreement still exists after the second and third opinion, an injured worker in the MPN may request an Independent Medical Review (IMR).

State Fee Schedule Guidelines

The state fee schedule is mandatory.

Medical Necessity and Medical Treatment Guidelines

Utilization review (UR) is the process used by employers or claims administrators to review treatment to determine if it is medically necessary. All employers or their workers' compensation claims administrators are required by law to have a UR program. This program is used to decide whether or not to approve medical treatment recommended by a physician, which must be based on the medical treatment guidelines.

Permanent Impairment Rating

The Disability Evaluation Unit, under the direction and authority of the Administrative Director, will issue permanent disability ratings as required under the subchapter utilizing the Schedule for Rating Permanent Disabilities. The Disability Evaluation Unit will prepare the following kinds of rating determinations:
1) Formal rating determinations
2) Summary rating determinations
3) Consultative rating determinations
4) Informal rating determinations.

These rating guidelines are pre-set and uniform throughout the state. The rating percentage is then converted to a monetary amount also in accordance with a pre-set schedule.

COLORADO

Colorado Department of Labor and Employment
Workers' Compensation
633 17th Street, Suite 400
Denver, CO 80202
Telephone: (888) 390-7936 (toll free) or (303) 318-8700
Fax: (303) 318-8710

State Website:

www.colorado.gov/cs/Satellite/CDLE-WorkComp/CDLE/1240336932511

State Rules and Regulations for Case Management

The state allows for managed care services which regulate medical provider choice and utilization review. The managed care services must be offered through a network or a preferred provider network.

Vocational Rehabilitation Services

A vendor will be considered qualified by the Director if the vendor has the services of a consultant who is registered with the Division or can demonstrate one of the following credentials:

The individual is a Certified Rehabilitation Counselor under the guidelines of the Commission on Rehabilitation Counselor Certification or can demonstrate equivalent credentials.

The individual has a Master's degree in vocational rehabilitation or a related field or can demonstrate equivalent work experience.

The individual has a Bachelor's degree in vocational rehabilitation, guidance counseling, psychology, or a related field or can demonstrate equivalent work in a formal education. The individual must also have two years' experience as a practitioner in the field of vocational rehabilitation.

Submission and implementation of the vocational rehabilitation plan:

A vocational evaluation should be provided by a qualified rehabilitation vendor designated by the insurer, and by the division in consultation with the injured worker. A vocational rehabilitation plan is required after an injured worker is determined to be an eligible employee to receive vocational rehabilitation services. Once the vocational plan is developed, it should be submitted to the division for approval within forty-five days of eligibility determination. In developing the rehabilitation plan, the rehabilitation vendor's goal is to strive to return the injured worker to suitable gainful employment.

Access to Medical Care

In all cases of injury, the employer or insurer is required to provide a list of medical providers to each injured worker. The list of medical providers is an approved panel of physicians designed to treat the employer's injured workers. The list must represent at maximum two physicians or two corporate medical providers or at minimum, one physician and one corporate medical provider. The panel list must be made available to the injured worker to help them make their selection in a treating physician.

If the services of a panel physician are not available at the time of the injury, the injured worker may elect to seek medical care from another non-panel physician or chiropractor. An injured worker may obtain a one-time change in the designated authorized treating physician that meets the state ninety day rule before the injured worker reaches maximum medical improvement.

State Fee Schedule Guidelines

Fee schedule is mandatory. Bill review is not mandatory.

Medical Necessity and Medical Treatment Guidelines

The medical provider is required to prepare a diagnosis-based treatment plan that includes specific treatment goals with expected time frames for completion in all cases where treatment falls within the scope of the medical treatment guidelines continues beyond six weeks.

The medical provider is required to supply a copy of the treatment plan to the injured worker and to the insurer, within fourteen days of request by any party. Should the injured worker require care that deviates from the state approved medical treatment guidelines; the medical provider shall supply the patient and the payer with a written explanation of the medical necessity for such care.

Permanent Impairment Rating

Where the authorized treating physician has determined that the injured worker is at maximum medical improvement (MMI) and has not returned to his/her pre-injury physical and/or mental state, the treating physician is required to determine if the cause is related to a permanent medical impairment.

The state established a Level II accreditation for physicians who make determinations regarding physical impairment ratings that must be in accordance with their administrative, legal, and medical roles.

CONNECTICUT

State of Connecticut Workers' Compensation Commission
Capitol Place
21 Oak Street
Hartford, CT 06106
Telephone: (860) 493-1500
Fax: (860) 247-1361

State Website: wcc.state.ct.us

State Rules and Regulations for Case Management

Rehabilitation nurses and nurse case managers employed by the employer in general play an important role in determining that an injured worker receives appropriate medical treatment and is returned to productive work as reasonably as possible. Healthcare professionals should be sensitive in understanding that there is the potential for a conflict of interest to ensue. There are some cases where disputes may arise between the injured worker and the insurer and the positions of these parties become adversarial.

The rehabilitation nurse or nurse case manager must be sensitive to the potential of a conflict of interest and refrain from engaging in any activity that could create accusations of partisanship. The injured worker has the right to determine the level of involvement of a rehabilitation nurse and/or nurse case manager in all treatment aspects of their case. The injured worker determines whether to allow the rehabilitation nurse or nurse care manager to attend the physician's examination or consultation. The Commission has the final determination in resolving disputes whenever they arise.

Vocational Rehabilitation Services

As provided in the general statutes, a disabled employee may be eligible for vocational rehabilitation benefits, provided the following statues are met:

The injured worker, employer, insurance carrier, physician, commissioner, or other interested parties may request vocational rehabilitation services by completing and filing an application signed by the applicant for vocational rehabilitation benefits.

To obtain approval from the commission to receive rehabilitation services, a permanent impairment must exist which substantially determines that the injured worker is disabled from performing their pre-injury job.

Access to Medical Care

An injured worker may choose a medical provider from an approved panel list of medical providers of the Workers' Compensation Commission who are licensed to practice in Connecticut, including practitioners of: chiropractic, medicine, naturopathy, optometry, osteopathy, and podiatry.

An injured worker may choose another treating physician even after an initial visit with an employer-designated medical provider.

When communicating with an injured worker, or his/her representative, or his/her treating physician, the nurse case manager or adjuster is required to identify him/herself as representing the employer or its insurance carrier.

The nurse case manager or adjuster must obtain the injured employee's written or verbal consent prior to attending a medical provider examination with them.

State Fee Schedule Guidelines

The state fee schedule is mandatory. Bill review is not mandated.

Medical Necessity and Medical Treatment Guidelines

Utilization review is required when there is a managed care plan in place.

Permanent Impairment Ratings

When an injured worker suffers a permanent disability as a result of a work-related injury or illness, he or she may receive Permanent Partial Disability. This benefit serves as compensation for the injured worker having suffered a permanent and partial disability to some part(s) of the body. A benefit determination is made in accordance to the date of the injury or illness which resulted in the permanent disability, which includes the part(s) of the body affected.

If the treating medical provider determines that the injured worker has reached Maximum Medical Improvement (MMI), and that the injured worker has sustained a permanent partial loss of use of a body part an issuance of a percentage disability rating would be appropriate. An assignment of an impairment disability rating marks the end of other workers' compensation benefits and makes the injured worker eligible to receive weekly PPD benefits for a specific number of weeks.

DELAWARE

State of Delaware Office of Workers' Compensation
4425 North Market Street, Third Floor
Wilmington, DE 19802
Telephone: (302) 761-8200
Fax: (302) 761-6601

State Websites: dia.delawareworks.com/workers-comp

State Rules and Regulations for Case Management

A provider of medical case management must be certified in the state of Delaware Office of Worker's Compensation.

Vocational Rehabilitation Services

A Vocational Rehabilitation Counselor's goal is to help injured workers achieve successful re-employment. Individuals interested in seeking re-employment are:

1) Assigned to work with a trained Vocational Rehabilitation Counselor,
2) Assisted in deciding the appropriate re-employment goal through reviewing their medical and work history, education, test results, and interest and abilities,
3) Encouraged to develop individualized plan to obtain their desired job.

Access to Medical Care

The injured worker can choose a treating physician. There is a physician panel list of certified medical providers that the injured worker is encouraged to choose from. If a private physician is selected a pre-authorization for services is required.

Any employee who alleges an industrial injury has the right to employ a physician, surgeon, dentist, optometrist or chiropractor of the employee's own choosing. The employee must notify the employer or its insurance carrier or to the board of their selection. If the alleged injury is determined to be compensable, the employer is liable for the reasonable cost of medical services of any physician, surgeon, dentist, optometrist or chiropractor whose employment was utilized by the injured worker.

State Fee Schedule Guidelines

Use of utilization review is mandatory. The Department of Labor has developed a utilization review program with the intent of providing reference for employers, insurance carriers, and health care providers for evaluation of medical necessity and charges. The intent of utilization review services is to provide a resolution on issues related to medical treatment and fee compliance with the health care payment system or medical practice guidelines on compensable claims. Compliance with the utilization review program should eliminate the employer or its insurance carrier's need for legal representation for issues related to cost.

An employer or insurance carrier may secure utilization review services to evaluate the quality, reasonableness and/or medical necessity of proposed or provided health care services. An agent conducting a utilization review program is required to contract with the Office of Workers' Compensation must certify that they are in compliance with the Utilization Review Accreditation Commission (URAC).

Medical Necessity and Medical Treatment Guidelines

If the medical provider has no current practice guidelines available to the health care provided, a party may file a petition with the Industrial Accident Board seeking a determination of the appropriateness of treatment.

Permanent Impairment Rating

Injured workers are paid permanent impairment disability (PPD) benefits for any permanent disability suffered as the result of an on-the-job injury. The treating physicians normally use the fifth edition of the American Medical Association (AMA) Guides to the Evaluation of Permanent Impairment.

The state Worker's Compensation office may provide for lump sum settlements for injured workers who have incurred permanent injuries on the job. The amount and extent of the recovery will vary depending upon the area of the body affected, the degree of permanent injury, and the injured worker's average weekly wage.

Permanency Rating—this is the percentage assigned by the doctor during the permanency evaluation. It represents the percentage of function the injured worker has lost in the injured body part. The doctor determines this number according to the specific guidelines published by the American Medical Association. Doctors can differ on this to some extent.

DISTRICT OF COLUMBIA

District of Columbia Department of Employment Services
Labor Standards Bureau
Office of Workers' Compensation
64 New York Avenue, NE, 2nd floor
Washington, DC 20002
Telephone: (202) 671-1000

State Website: does.dc.gov/does/cwp/view,a,1232,q,537428.asp

State Rules and Regulations for Case Management

The state Vocational Rehabilitation Service requires that vocational rehabilitation counselors design a plan, within reason, to return the injured worker to employment at a wage as close as possible to the wage that the injured worker earned at the time of injury. Employers will file vocational rehabilitation plans with the Office of Workers' Compensation. The Office of Worker's Compensation will monitor the vocational rehabilitation services to determine is the services are adequately beneficial to the injured worker. An injured worker may submit an application for vocational rehabilitation services or request to change service providers.

Access to Medical Care

The injured worker has the right to choose a treating physician to provide medical care. If the employee is unable to select a physician and the injury requires immediate medical care, the employer shall select a physician for the injured worker. Where medically indicated or at the advice of the injured worker, the attending physician may consult with the injured worker's personal physician.

State Fee Schedule Guidelines

The state fee schedule is not mandatory.

Medical Necessity and Medical Treatment Guidelines

Any medical care or services provided are subject to utilization review. Utilization review may be accomplished prospectively, concurrently, or retrospectively. A utilization review organization or agent shall be certified by the Utilization Review Accreditation Commission (URAC).

The injured worker, employer, or insurance carrier may initiate the review, accepting the diagnosis of injury is correct, where it appears that the medical necessity, character or sufficiency of medical services is improper or clarification is needed on medical service that is scheduled to be provided.

Permanent Impairment Rating

Use of impairment rating guidelines are not mandated; but the most recent edition of the American Medical Association's *Guides to the Evaluation of Permanent Impairment* may be utilized in determining permanent impairment.

FLORIDA

Florida Department of Financial Services
Division of Workers' Compensation
200 East Gaines Street
Tallahassee, FL 32399
Telephone: (850) 413-1601

State Website: www.myfloridacfo.com/wc

State Rules and Regulations for Case Management

The state Qualified Rehabilitation Provider (QRP) requirements for a Rehabilitation Nurse include:
1) Current Florida RN license,
2) Current CRRN, COHN, CRC, CDMS, or CCM certificate,
3) Current e-mail address, and
4) Verification of a completed department-sponsored workshop.

The QRP requirements for a Rehabilitation Counselor include:
1) Current CRC or CDMS certificate,
2) Current e-mail address, and
3) Verification of a completed department-sponsored training.

The Limitations of Practice for a QRP
1) A licensed practical nurse does not qualify as a QRP.
2) Only a nurse licensed in the state of Florida as a registered professional nurse and who provides proof of one of the accepted professional credentials may apply to become a QRP and be listed in the directory.

Vocational Rehabilitation Services

Provide appropriate and necessary re-employment services to assist injured employees in their return to suitable gainful employment.

Educate carriers about requirements for reviewing cases and providing medical care coordination and re-employment services.

Access to Medical Care

The employer is required to select a treating medical physician. The injured worker must provide a written request to the employer or the carrier for one change of physician during the course of treatment. Once a change of physician is granted, the originally authorized physician services shall be cancelled by the employer or carrier. If the carrier fails to provide a change of physician as requested by the injured worker, the injured worker may select the physician. All services will be considered authorized if treatment is determined to be compensable and medically necessary.

State Fee Schedule Guidelines

The fee schedule is mandatory, unless there is a contract between parties to the claim.

Medical Necessity and Medical Treatment Guidelines

The state has mandatory utilization services that include reviewing for billing errors or overutilization of medical services. If an insurance carrier questions whether over-utilization of medical services or a billing error has occurred, or if a violation of treatment protocols occurs, it must disallow or adjust payment for such services in compliance with the rules adopted by the department.

Permanent Impairment Rating

In determining a Physical Impairment Rating, the American Medical Association's third edition *Guides to the Evaluation of Permanent Impairment.* The AMA is adopted as the schedule for determining the existence and degree of permanent impairment for all injuries prior to July 1, 1990.

For injuries occurring on or after its effective date, the *Florida Impairment Rating Guide,* which is adopted by reference as part of this rule, shall be used. The Florida Impairment Rating Guide, also known as the Florida Impairment Rating Schedule, is the "uniform permanent impairment rating schedule" and the "uniform disability rating schedule" referenced in Florida statutes. The impairment rating must always be applied to the body as a whole.

GEORGIA

Georgia State Board of Worker's Compensation
270 Peachtree Street, NW
Atlanta, Georgia GA 30303-1299
Telephone: (404) 656-2048

State Website: sbwc.georgia.gov/portal/site/SBWC

State Rules and Regulations for Case Management

Georgia Board Regulations require that medical case managers will have one of the following certifications:
1) Certified Rehabilitation Registered Nurse (CRRN), or
2) Certified Case Manager (CCM), or
3) Certified Occupational Health Nurse (COHN) or Certified Occupational Health Nurse Specialist (COHN-S)

Vocational Rehabilitation Services

A Rehabilitation Supplier should hold one of the certifications or licenses:
1) CRC—Certified Rehabilitation Counselor
2) CDMS—Certified Disability Management Specialist
3) CWAVES—Certified Work Adjustment & Vocational Evaluation Specialist
4) CRRN—Certified Registered Rehabilitation Nurse Program
5) LPC—Licensed Professional Counselor
6) CCM—Certified Case Manager
7) COHN—Certified Occupational Health Nurse
8) COHN-S—Certified Occupational Health Nurse - Specialist

Registration as a state Rehabilitation Supplier is a requirement to provide case management. A separate Catastrophic Rehabilitation Certification is required to provide case management services for catastrophic injury cases.

Vocational Rehabilitation services by a Board Registered Rehabilitation Supplier are required in claims where the injury is catastrophic and for non-catastrophic claims with dates of injury prior to July 1, 1992.

The state requires that the medical case manager coordinates health care throughout the continuum of required care to achieve the highest level of quality medical care in the most cost-effective and expedited ways possible. The primary purpose of case management is to advocate for the injured worker by coordinating care, minimizing complications, and establishing a return to work plan through ongoing assessments.

The case manager is able to provide a high quality of care in a timely manner by using the basic case management functions of assessing, planning, implementing, monitoring, and evaluating outcomes. Case managers are responsible for facilitating communication between all parties to the claim, such as: the injured worker or their representative, employer, employer's representative, insurer, or health care provider.

The case manager must act as an advocate for the injured worker in the medical management process. The case manager should:

1) Provide assistance and information to the injured worker regarding medical issues.
2) Ensure a high quality of medical care in a cost-effective manner.
3) Immediately triage of cases and prompt evaluation and assignment of appropriate medical case management depending on the nature of the injury and the level of complexity of medical case management needs.
4) Identify medical or return to work issues to minimize medical and disability costs.
5) Consult with medical providers to determine appropriate levels of medical case management intervention.
6) Assure efficient and timely service delivery to help the injured worker reach maximum medical recovery and return to work as soon as medically appropriate.

In cases where an injured worker is represented by an attorney, the rehab supplier cannot contact the injured workers unless permission is granted by the attorney on record. A special state provision allows case managers employed by third party administrators, insurers, and employers to perform activities in the administration of their worker's compensation claims handling without attorney consent.

Access to Medical Care

Employers must post a Panel of Physicians consisting of a minimum of six doctors. The injured worker may select one of these six physicians. The Board may grant exceptions to the required size of the panel where it is demonstrated that six physicians or groups of physicians are not reasonably accessible. The panel must include one orthopedic physician and not more than two industrial clinics. Wherever possible, a minority physician must be included. The injured worker may make one change to another doctor on the list without the permission of their employer.

State Fee Schedule Guidelines

The state fee schedule is mandatory.

Medical Necessity and Medical Treatment Guidelines

Medical treatment disputes may be addressed through the utilization review process. Internal dispute resolution with a thirty day time frame is available for any party of who does not agree with the utilization review outcome. Additionally, any party may request the board to intervene if the medical treatment dispute remains unresolved after thirty days. Utilization review is not mandatory.

Permanent Impairment Rating

Weekly benefits based are based on the type and extent of permanent disability. The authorized treating physician determines impairment ratings based upon *Guides to the Evaluation of Permanent Impairment,* fifth edition, published by the American Medical Association (AMA).

HAWAII

Hawaii Department of Labor and Industrial Relations
Honolulu Claims Office
830 Punchbowl Street
Honolulu, HI 96813
Telephone: (808) 586-8970
Fax: (808) 586-8980

State Website: hawaii.gov/labor

State Rules and Regulations for Case Management

Hawaii does not mandate medical case management services, but offers medical treatment guidelines as cost-saving measures.

Vocational Rehabilitation Services

The state Vocational Rehabilitation Services requires that a vocational rehabilitation specialist register and certify as a provider of vocational rehabilitation services to practice.

The purposes of vocational rehabilitation is to restore an injured worker's earnings capacity as nearly as possible to that level that the worker was earning at the time of injury and to return the injured worker to suitable gainful employment in the active labor force as quickly as possible in a cost-effective manner.

The state regulations require that the initial evaluation be conducted prior to submittal of vocational rehabilitation plan. A provider must submit an initial evaluation report of the injured worker to the state and employer within forty-five days from the date of the referral. The evaluation should determine whether the injured worker requires vocational rehabilitation services to return to work, and will also identify a suitable employer.

The injured worker may select and initiate services with a certified rehabilitation provider based on state statues. All subsequent plan changes or transfers of rehabilitation provider should be in accordance with state statutes.

A rehabilitation counselor seeking registration with the state as a registered rehabilitation specialist shall apply to the director. The applicant may be registered if the director finds the applicant has a current certification by the Commission on Rehabilitation Counselor Certification as a certified rehabilitation counselor.

Access to Medical Care

The injured worker may obtain treatment from a physician of his or her choice. The injured worker may only be under the care with one treating physician. The injured worker's treating physician may refer them to other specialist(s) with the approval of the employer's insurance carrier.

The injured worker may change the treating physician once, but must notify the insurance carrier before making the change. Any other changes in physician will require approval from the insurance carrier before the change occurs.

If an injured worker changes or transfers to another medical provider, such a transfer must be submitted in writing to the director. In such instances, the latter medical provider is entitled to all considerations granted to the former medical provider. The latter medical provider shall be compensated for all services performed after the date of the case transfer.

After the initial medical provider selection, any subsequent changes or transfers of medical providers shall be made by the state director, unless there is an agreement made between the employer and injured worker.

State Fee Schedule Guidelines

The state fee schedule is mandatory. Billing cost review follows the medical fee schedule.

Medical Necessity and Medical Treatment Guidelines

The state regulates guidelines for the frequency and duration of treatments for reasonably medically necessary services. The use of treatment guidelines cannot interfere with the injured workers' rights to receive medical care.

Permanent Impairment Rating

Maximum medical improvement or medical stabilization is defined by board rules as not needing further medical care or treatment. Medical stabilization also occurs when the injured worker refuses further treatment or care from the medical provider.

After the injured worker reaches the point of medical stability or maximum medical recovery, he or she may be referred to a physician for a permanent impairment rating evaluation. The evaluation will be used to determine the amount of Permanent Partial Disability (PPD) awarded.

Physicians are authorized to evaluate permanent impairment. Physicians are defined by workers 'compensation law as doctors of medicine, dentists, chiropractors, osteopaths, naturopaths, psychologists, optometrists, and podiatrists. Final disability ratings are not based solely on medical impairment ratings.

Objective guidelines are used for the determination of medical impairment ratings, such as: state approval; the most recent edition of the AMA Guides, the Diagnostic and Statistical Manual of Mental Disorders III(R), and the Orthopedic Surgeons Rating Manual for medical impairment rating evaluations.

PPD benefits are limited to a certain number of weeks for payments. Specifically, scheduled injuries are limited to the number of weeks for each injured body part times the maximum weekly benefit for the year of the injury.

IDAHO

State of Idaho Industrial Commission
700 S. Clearwater Lane
Boise, Idaho 83712
Telephone: (800) 950-2110 (toll free, outside Boise) or (208) 334-6000
Toll Free (outside Boise): (800) 950-2110
Fax: (208) 334-2321

State Website: iic.idaho.gov

State Rules and Regulations for Case Management
Idaho has not established a case management state plan but does endorse use of rehabilitation services as a form of workers' compensation managed care.

Vocational Rehabilitation Services

The state Vocational Rehabilitation Services requires that rehabilitation consultants be employees of the Idaho Industrial Commission, which is responsible for ensuring injured workers receive the benefits the law requires. Rehabilitation consultants will assist the injured worker in returning to work based on their transferable job skills. State rehabilitation consultants are not employees of the insurance companies, attorneys, or other groups involved in the workers' compensation process. The rehabilitation consultant is considered a neutral professional third party who provides objective return to work assistance to the injured worker.

Work-related injuries can result in devastating medical indemnity costs for the employer as well as extended medical recovery time for the injured worker. The goal of rehabilitation services is to help the injured worker return to their pre-injury job or a similar job at their pre-injury wage status. The rehabilitation division interviews the injured worker, employer, medical provider to develop a vocational plan which is designed to expedite a return to work for injured worker. The rehabilitation services are provided at no additional cost to the employer, insurer, or injured worker.

A rehabilitation plan should include:
- Establishing a transitional-duty work program
- Identifying transitional-duty work positions
- Matching injured worker's capabilities to their physical and medical conditions
- Preparing an injured worker for a work position, if indicated

Access to Medical Care

The employer has the responsibility to provide adequate medical care for an injured worker at the time of an accident. If the initial treating physician has been selected by the employer, it is expected for that physician to provide reasonable medical care. If there is no designated treating physician, the injured worker may select the treating physician of his or her choice for the initial treatment.

If the injured worker requests to change physicians, he or she can obtain a referral from the treating physician or request a change of physicians. If the injured worker's request is denied, the injured worker can file a request for a Change of Physician with the Idaho Industrial Commission.

State Fee Schedule Guidelines

The Idaho Industrial Commission has adopted a permanent fee schedule governing payments for medical services under the Idaho Workers' Compensation Law. There are no requirements or mandates for utilization review. Medical providers shall utilize the medical fee schedule to analyze its cost-effectiveness.

Idaho is a zero-deductible state for workers' compensation medical charges. No portion of the unpaid medical bill is to be paid by the injured worker on claims accepted by the insurer.

Medical Necessity and Medical Treatment Guidelines

Medical charges are paid based on the Idaho Code and the fee scheduled administered by the Industrial Commission. If a bill is reduced to comply with the usual and customary rates, the injured worker or employer is not responsible for the balance of the charges. An injured worker will be responsible, however, for non-covered expenses or charges unrelated to a work-related injury.

If there are questions regarding a medical diagnosis, medical treatment, medical stability, or a permanent partial impairment, an independent medical evaluation (IME) may be scheduled with a physician or a panel of physicians.

Permanent Impairment Rating

An evaluation for a permanent disability rating is an appraisal of the injured worker's present and probable future ability to engage in gainful activity as it is affected by the medical factor of permanent impairment and by pertinent non-medical factors.

The percentage of Permanent Partial Disability (PPD) is determined by the Industrial Commission and is dependent upon the facts of the case. Benefits are paid at 55 percent of the average state wage at the time of the injury for a specified number of weeks, based on the percentage of the disability award.

ILLINOIS

Illinois Worker's Compensation Commission (IWCC)
Chicago Office
100 W. Randolph, Suite 8-200
Chicago, IL 60601
Telephone: (312) 814-6611

State Website: www.iwcc.il.

State Rules and Regulations for Case Management

The state does not mandate managed care services.

Vocational Rehabilitation Services

Vocational rehabilitation is a required service to be provided by an employer when it is necessary to return an injured worker to gainful employment post-recovery from an on-the-job injury. Vocational rehabilitation may include the injured worker receiving job counseling, supervision of a job search, resume building, and vocational educational retraining at an accredited learning institution. If the injured worker cannot return to his or her pre-injury job, the employer must pay for treatment, instruction, and training necessary for the physical, mental, and vocational rehabilitation of the injured worker. The injured worker is required to cooperate in an assigned rehabilitation program. The injured worker may select a provider for vocational rehabilitation services or may accept the services of a provider selected by the employer.

Access to Medical Care

The employer must maintain a panel list of physicians and make that list accessible to the employees. An injured worker has the option of selecting a physician from the employer's listed panel. The injured worker may also choose an alternate physician from the panel if dissatisfied with the initial physician choice.

Upon agreement between the employer and the injured worker, the injured worker may select his own medical provider and hospital services at the employer's expense.

If the Illinois Workers' Compensation Commission determines that a treating physician is rendering improper or inadequate care, the commission may order the injured worker to select another qualified physician. If the injured worker refuses to change treating physicians, the commission may determine that the employer is not responsible for payment of the physician's charges.

State Fee Schedule Guidelines

Medical providers are paid according to the fee schedule, which is a part of the state's cost containment. The fee schedule applies to medical treatments and procedures that are rendered on or after February 1, 2006, and are covered under the Illinois Workers' Compensation Act.

The Illinois Worker's Compensation Act will cover medical care that is less than the lesser cost of the health care provider's actual charge or the fee schedule amount, unless the employer/insurer and health care provider have entered into a contract for a different reimbursement rate.

Medical Necessity and Medical Treatment Guidelines

The state uses a utilization system to evaluate medical necessity that is based on medical health care standards or nationally recognized peer review guidelines, as well as nationally recognized evidence based standards as provided in this Act. Utilization review techniques may include prospective review, second opinions, concurrent review, discharge planning, peer review, independent medical examinations, and retrospective review.

Permanent Impairment Rating

When the employee has sustained an injury or industrial disease which results in a permanent disability, additional benefits are provided to the injured worker. The circumstances under which these benefits are payable and the method of determining the amount of the benefit are based on the statute. Claims may be settled between the employer and the injured worker directly or through their representatives, provided the settlements are approved by the Industrial Commission.

Illinois has adopted use of the sixth edition of the AMA Guide on permanent impairment ratings for injuries dating September 1, 2011 and after.

INDIANA

Indiana Board of Workers Compensation
Worker's Compensation Board of Indiana
402 West Washington Street Room W-196
Indianapolis, Indiana IN 46204
Telephone: (800) 824-COMP

State Website: www.in.gov/wcb

State Rules and Regulations for Case Management
The state does not mandate case management services. Insurance carriers may hire rehabilitation nurses to manage the medical treatment of an injured worker.

Vocational Rehabilitation Services
　　If an injured worker is unable to return to their pre-injury work, they may be eligible to receive vocational rehabilitation services. Under the Indiana Worker's Compensation Act the employer is not required to pay for private vocational rehabilitation services.
　　Vocational rehabilitation nurses may be helpful in coordinating successful medical treatment for the injured worker. Only the physician can ask the rehabilitation professional to leave the examination room at any time and the professional is required to comply.
　　Upon receipt of the report of injury, the local office of vocational rehabilitation shall, provide the injured employee with a written explanation of:
- Available rehabilitation services available to the injured employee; and
- The application process by which the injured employee may make application for those services
- The vocational rehabilitation office shall determine the injured worker's eligibility for appropriate rehabilitation services.
- The vocational rehabilitation office shall implement the rehabilitation plan. After completion of the rehabilitation program, the injured worker shall be provided with job placement services to the rehabilitated employee.

Access to Medical Care

The employer and insurance carrier have the right to direct the medical care of the injured worker in Indiana, with few exceptions. In some cases, an employer may provide a physician, free of charge, for the medical care of an employee's injuries.

An injured worker may be referred to the nearest urgent care treatment facility, for an employer or carrier selecting a medical provider for follow-up care. If an injured worker obtains emergency medical care without the prior approval of his or her employer or insurance carrier, it is the injured workers responsibility to notify the carrier or employer. The injured worker has the right to obtain medical care that is at the expense of the employer.

State Fee Schedule Guidelines

There is no mandatory state fee schedule or utilization review plan currently in place.

Medical Necessity and Medical Treatment Guidelines

Utilization review is not mandatory. Workers' compensation and occupational disease cases are decided on by the facts of the individual case as a whole. While an unreasonable denial or unreasonable delay of necessary medical treatment could result in penalties, employing utilization review will not, standing alone, justify penalties.

Permanent Impairment Rating

An award of a Permanent Partial Impairment (PPI) can only be made after it is determined that the injured worker has reached "maximum medical improvement" (MMI), which means that the injury has recovered to the fullest extent possible and no further medical care is needed. In other words, the injured worker is stated to be as good as he will get after completing all medical care, post work-related injury. When the injured worker meets maximum medical improvement, temporary total disability benefits will be terminated and a Permanent Partial Impairment (PPI) rating may be assessed by the treating physician or another physician.

PPI as it is referred to, means the partial or total loss of the function of a body part or the body as a whole. In Indiana, compensation for impairment is paid according to a statutory schedule. For injuries occurring on and after July 1, 1991, the calculation of impairment compensation is not based on the employee's wages. Rather, impairment awards are designed strictly to compensate the injured worker for the loss or loss of use of body parts or functions.

An injured worker's PPI is most often assessed by the treating physician. Physicians use the sixth edition of the American Medical Association's *Guides to the Evaluation of Permanent Impairment* in evaluating the employee's impairment rating. A PPI rating is stated by the physician in terms of a percentage of loss or loss of use of a body part or the whole body.

IOWA

Iowa Division of Workers Compensation
1000 East Grand Avenue
Des Moines, Iowa 50319-0209
Telephone: (515) 281-5387 or (800) JOB-IOWA (toll free)

State Website: www.iowaworkforce.org/wc

State Rules and Regulations for Case Management

Iowa has not established a case management state plan but does endorse use of vocational rehabilitation services as a cost containment measure.

Vocational Rehabilitation Services

The stated mission of the Iowa Vocational Rehabilitation Services is to work for and with individuals who have disabilities to achieve their employment, independence, and economic goals.

Rehabilitation Counselors are required to participate in a two-day orientation at the Division Central Office. Counselors are coached by Area Supervisors and VR Counselors to achieve competency in a number of casework activities.

Access to Medical Care

The employer provides medical care reasonably suited to treat the employee's injury, and has the right to choose the treating medical care provider.

If the employee is dissatisfied with the care offered, the employee should discuss the problem with the employer or insurance carrier. In certain situations the employee may wish to request alternate care. If the employer, or insurance carrier, does not allow alternate care, the employee (through appropriate proceedings) may apply to the Workers' Compensation Commissioner for alternate medical care.

State Fee Schedule Guidelines

There is no mandatory state fee schedule or utilization review. The employer must pay for all reasonable and necessary medical care required for treating the employee's injury.

Medical Necessity and Medical Treatment Guidelines

Utilization review is not mandatory.

Iowa may assign a monitor to ensure that injured workers are able to access quality care and that utilization patterns are tracked and costs fall within acceptable standards of practice. If over utilization or underutilization is apparent or quality of management service is inadequate, efforts should be made to determine the issue and resolution of the problem.

The board has established a utilization division for the purpose of providing a mechanism for review of questions related to:
1) Appropriateness of levels of nursing care.
2) Documentation of the credentials of the nurse(s) offering the service(s).
3) Documentation of the care provided.
4) Documentation of the costs of nursing services provided by certified registered nurses as requested by users and payers of such services.

Permanent Impairment Rating

The *Guides to the Evaluation of Permanent Impairment*, fifth edition, published by the American Medical Association are adopted as a guide for determining permanent partial disabilities under Iowa Code. The percentage of permanent impairment may be determined by use of the Fifth Edition of the guides, and payment of weekly compensation for permanent partial scheduled injuries should be made based on this determination. The worker's compensation commissioner must approve all payments related to impairment rating determination verifying compliance by the employer or insurance carrier with the Iowa Workers' Compensation Act. The state impairment rule does not prevent introduction of additional medical opinions or evidence in establishing the percentage of permanent disability to which the injured worker would be entitled.

KANSAS

Kansas Department of Labor
Division of Workers Compensation
800 SW Jackson, Suite 600
Topeka, Kansas 66612
Telephone: (800) 332-0353 (toll free)

State Website: www.dol.ks.gov/wc/about.html

State Rules and Regulations for Case Management
The state has no mandated managed care guidelines.

Vocational Rehabilitation Services

The primary purpose of the workers compensation act is to restore the injured worker to work at a comparable wage.

Vocational Rehabilitation qualifications as a counselor, evaluator, and job placement specialist are listed below. Each professional seeking to qualify as a vocational rehabilitation counselor for cases under the Kansas workers compensation act shall have:

- A master's degree from a nationally accredited program in rehabilitation counselor education; or
- A master's degree in counseling, guidance and counseling, clinical psychology, counseling psychology, clinical social work or any related field which includes nine hours of graduate course work in counseling; and
- One year of experience as a vocational rehabilitation counselor or completion of a nationally accredited rehabilitation counselor internship program from a college or university.

Insurance carriers and/or employers shall furnish to the selected vocational rehabilitation vendor or all medical records that may be necessary to make an effective, informed vocational rehabilitation determination. Vocational rehabilitation vendors are required to comply with the state's standards of conduct for vocational rehabilitation professionals.

No vocational assessment, evaluation, services, or training should be provided or made available under the workers compensation act unless specifically agreed to by the employer or insurance carrier providing or making available such assessment, evaluation, services or training.

After all parties to the claim agree to providing rehabilitation services, the vocational rehabilitation administrator may make recommendations for and supervise such assessment, evaluation, services or training on behalf of the employee. Such assessment, evaluation, services or training should not be arbitrarily terminated by the employer or insurance carrier once such an agreement is entered into.

Access to Medical Care

The employer/insurance carrier has the right to select an authorized treating provider. The injured worker may select a medical provider from the employer's list of three, who may become the authorized treating medical care provider. If the injured worker is unable to obtain satisfactory services from any of the medical care providers submitted by the employer, either party may request the director to select a treating medical care provider.

If an injured worker files an application that the services of the medical care provider are not satisfactory, the director may authorize the appointment of some other health care provider. In such cases, the employer may submit the names of three medical care providers who are not associated in practice together.

State Fee Schedule Guidelines
The state fee schedule is mandatory.

Medical Necessity and Medical Treatment Guidelines

There is no mandatory utilization review. The division uses, "The Official Disability Guidelines Treatment in Workers Compensation" (ODG/TWC), published by Work Loss Data Institute (WLDI). The ODG/TWC medical treatment guide is the primary standard of reference in determining the frequency and extent of services presumed to be medically necessary and appropriate for compensable injuries as stated under the Kansas Workers Compensation Act.

Permanent Impairment Rating

When permanent total disability results from an injury, weekly payments shall be made during the period of permanent total disability in a sum equal to 66 2/3 percent of the average gross weekly wage of the injured worker. The payment of compensation for permanent total disability shall continue for the duration of the disability, and is subject to review and modification. Kansas uses the fourth edition of the AMA Disability Guidelines for Assessment of Permanent Impairment Ratings.

KENTUCKY

Kentucky Department of Workers' Claims
657 Chamberlin Avenue
Frankfort, KY 40601
Telephone: (502) 564-5550

State Website: www.labor.ky.gov/workersclaims

State Rules and Regulations for Case Management

The state has adopted rules for a managed care network. Under the managed care network, case managers must be qualified as either a certified case manager, certified rehabilitation counselor, certified insurance rehabilitation specialist, or certified rehabilitation registered nurse who may oversee and monitor case management provisions of the managed care plan.

Vocational Rehabilitation Services

The purpose of Vocational Rehabilitation Services is to empower individuals with disabilities to maximize employment, achieve economic self-sufficiency and independence, and realize full inclusion and integration back into society.

Access to Medical Care

Employers are granted input into the matter of physician selection through managed care plans approved by the commission. Employees still have their choice of physician but within the confines of a provider network.

The injured worker may be allowed to obtain a second opinion, at the employer's expense, from an outside physician if a managed health care system physician recommends surgery.

Restrictions on network provider selection, which is imposed by a managed health care system, will not apply to emergency medical care needs.

State Fee Schedule Guidelines

The state fee schedule is mandatory.

Medical Necessity and Medical Treatment Guidelines

Cost containment and the administration of medically related services are the primary responsibility of the Department of Workers' Claims.

Compensable claims are subject to utilization review when any of the following occur:

- A medical provider requests pre-authorization of a medical treatment or procedure;
- Notification of a surgical procedure or a treatment plan is received;
- The total medical cost cumulatively exceeds $3,000;
- The total lost work days cumulatively exceed thirty days; or
- An administrative law judge orders a review.

These are minimum criteria. Some utilization review programs review additional claims based on the program's own internal review criteria.

Permanent Impairment Rating

It is the opinion of the commissioner that it is in the best interest of Kentucky workers and employers to continue the use of the fifth edition of the *Guides to the Evaluation of Permanent Impairment* in assessing impairment ratings pursuant to the Kentucky Workers' Compensation Act.

LOUISIANA

Louisiana Workforce Commission
Workers Compensation
3724 Government Street
Alexandria, LA 71302
Telephone: (318) 487-5966

State Website: www.ldol.state.la.us

State Rules and Regulations for Case Management

The state has no mandatory managed care provision, but utilizes bill and utilization review as cost containment initiatives.

Vocational Rehabilitation Services

Vocational Rehabilitation (VR) is a program that provides services to help injured workers with a disability obtain the job skills and other resources they need to keep a job, and/or develop a new career.

The Office of Workers' Compensation Administration requires vocational rehabilitation counselors to be licensed and it maintains a current listing of rehabilitation counselors licensed to practice rehabilitation services in the state of Louisiana.

State regulation requires that when an employee suffers a covered injury which precludes them from earning wages equal to their wages earned prior to the injury, the employee shall be entitled to prompt rehabilitation services provided by the carrier/employer.

If an injured worker is determined eligible for VR services, the injured worker and VR counselor will work together to develop an Individualized Plan for Employment (IPE). This plan is designed to assist the injured worker in preparing for and obtaining employment. Throughout the planning process, emphasis is placed on informing the injured worker of possible choices of vocational (work) goals, services, and providers of services.

Access to Medical Care

The injured worker has the discretion to select the treating physician, but the physician must be approved by the employer/insurance carrier to continue treatment beyond $750 worth of medical care unless the care is provided under emergency conditions. However, the employer/insurer withholding of such consent is not to be arbitrary and capricious or without probable cause.

The employer may require an injured worker to be examined by a physician of his or her choice. The injured worker's failure to submit to any reasonable examination may cause compensation payments to be temporarily suspended.

The injured worker has the freedom to choose his or her initial treating physician. However, the injured worker must obtain permission from the employer/insurer to switch from one physician specialist to another within the same specialty or field of practice.

State Fee Schedule Guidelines

State fee schedule is mandatory. The purpose of fee schedule rules is to establish and implement effective injury control measures.

Medical Necessity and Medical Treatment Guidelines

Utilization review is mandatory. The utilization review rules require the use of appropriate procedures to establish standards of care in determining the medical necessity for hospital care or services, medical or surgical care, or any non-medical care recognized by the laws of the state.

All non-emergency hospital admissions must be pre-certified with an appropriate length of stay assigned. Continued hospital stay review must also be performed on each approved admission. Emergency hospital admission must meet specified criteria as outlined in the utilization review guidelines and must also have concurrent review performed. The rules also provide appropriate procedures to be followed when seeking approval to continue treatment beyond the statutory limit of $750.

Permanent Impairment Rating

State statutes mandate that the most recent version of the AMA Guidelines should be utilized in permanent impairment rating determinations.

Temporary disability benefits paid shall include such period as may be reasonably required for training or education under a rehabilitation program approved by the state.

MAINE

Maine Workers Compensation Board
27 State House Station
Augusta, ME 04333-0027
Telephone: (207) 287-3751
Fax: (207) 287-7198

State Website: www.maine.gov/wcb

State Rules and Regulations for Case Management

The state has not endorsed a mandatory managed care service, but has adopted standards for vocational rehabilitation services.

Vocational Rehabilitation Services

The Maine Workers' Compensation Board may refer an injured worker to a board-approved facility for evaluation of vocational rehabilitation services, treatment, or training necessary and appropriate to return the injured worker to suitable employment.

A board-approved facility is defined as a facility in which those providing direct services to an injure worker have at least minimum qualifications of:
1) A Bachelor's degree in Rehabilitation Counseling or a closely related field with five years of experience in the profession of Rehabilitation Counseling; or
2) A Certified Rehabilitation Counseling (CRC); or
3) A Master's degree in Rehabilitation Counseling or a closely related field.

Access to Medical Care

The employer has the option of selecting the initial treating physician. An injured worker being treated by a medical care provider selected by the employer's may submit to all reasonable care during the continuance of disability if services are requested by the employer. The injured worker may submit to an examination by a physician, surgeon, or chiropractor authorized to practice under the laws of Maine. The services selected will be reimbursed by the employer.

The injured worker may petition the employer or board to request a one-time change to a medical provider or a medical specialist. The employer would be responsible for payment for this medical treatment.

State Fee Schedule Guidelines

The state fee schedule is mandatory. A service is subject to the maximum allowable payment if it conforms to a description contained in the medical fee schedule. If a dispute ensues regarding medical bill payment and/or medical service provisions, the employer may be required to pay the medical bill amount.

Medical Necessity and Medical Treatment Guidelines

Utilization Review (UR) Agents providing or performing UR services shall utilize Treatment Guidelines approved by the Workers' Compensation Board. The UR agent must be certified by the American Utilization Accreditation Commission (URAC) to provide UR state approved services.

Permanent Impairment Rating

Once a permanent injury is established, the injured worker may seek a permanent impairment evaluation. Permanent impairment rating determinations are required to be performed by a qualified specialist based on their training and/or experience to perform permanent impairment evaluations. The specialist's fee for calculating the permanent impairment rating must be paid by the employer/insurer.

In cases that involve a permanent injury, the employer/insurer and/or injured worker are required to submit a permanent impairment rating. Permanent impairment ratings are not binding if disputed. If the permanent impairment rating is disputed, it is not necessary to submit it until the case settles or the dispute is resolved.

Before the state approves a lump sum settlement, a permanent impairment rating or a report from a qualified health care provider stating there is no permanent injury must be obtained. Maine uses the fourth edition of the AMA *Guides*.

MARYLAND

State of Maryland
Workers' Compensation Commission
10 East Baltimore Street
Baltimore, Maryland MD 21202-1641
Telephone: (410) 864-5100 or Toll-Free (800) 492-0479 (toll free outside metro Baltimore)

State Website: www.wcc.state.md.us

State Rules and Regulations for Case Management

Maryland has not established a case management state plan but does endorse use of vocational rehabilitation services as a cost containment measure.

Vocational Rehabilitation Services

The Code of Maryland Labor and Employment Act requires that vocational rehabilitation practitioners register and vocational rehabilitation providers enroll with the Commission before providing vocational rehabilitation services to an eligible disabled or injured worker.

Rehabilitation practitioner means an individual who provides vocational rehabilitation services including:
1) a nurse certified by the State Board of Nursing as a nurse case manager;
2) a rehabilitation counselor;
3) a vocational evaluator;
4) a physical therapist and;
5) an occupational therapist.

Practitioners providing vocational rehabilitation services to more than three injured workers per year are required to register with the Workers' Compensation Commission.

Vocational Rehabilitation services are a workers' compensation benefit that provides a disabled eligible injured worker who cannot return to his former job as a result of work-related injury assistance in re-entering the workforce. A specialist in vocational rehabilitation provides services that may include testing, job placement, vocational counseling, on the job training, and retraining to the injured worker to enable them to return to work.

Access to Medical Care

The injured worker has the option to select their treating medical provider. If an injured worker cannot locate a medical provider who is willing to provide medical treatment based on the State Medical Fee Guide, the injured worker should request recommendations on securing a treating physician if none are available in their location. The insurer/employer is required to have a list of participating medical providers in the various areas of the state.

State Fee Schedule Guidelines

The state medical fee schedule is mandatory.

Medical Necessity and Medical Treatment Guidelines

There is no mandatory state utilization review or treatment guideline.

Permanent Impairment Rating

The state approves physician use of the fourth edition of the AMA Guides to evaluate impairment ratings of the injured worker's disability.

An injured worker requesting a lump sum payment based on their impairment rating must file an application with the commission. The application must be accompanied by all documents which support the injured worker's claim of permanent impairment.

The insurer or employer who may be required to make a lump sum payment must file a statement with the commission indicating they have an outstanding balance of payments due the injured worker or file a statement indicating whether they object to granting a lump sum payment.

A hearing on the application must be scheduled only if an objection or a request for hearings are filed, or on the commission's own initiative.

MASSACHUSETTS

Massachusetts Labor and Workforce Development
Public Information Office
Department of Industrial Accidents
1 Congress Street, Suite 100
Boston, MA 02114-2017
Telephone: (617) 727-4900, ext. 470

State Website: www.mass.gov/lwd

State Rules and Regulations for Case Management

The state has adopted a Preferred Provider Agreements (PPAs) which is governed by the Division of Insurance (DOI) to manage worker's compensation health care. Employers who contract with PPAs may require an injured worker be evaluated initially by a medical provider from a PPA. Injured workers have the option to select a treating medical provider outside the Health Maintenance Organization (HMO) and the Managed Care Organization (MCO) networks. The injured worker is only limited to their initial medical provider selection.

Vocational Rehabilitation Services

Vocational rehabilitation services may be provided to injured workers only by organizations approved by the state as qualified providers.

All vocational rehabilitation providers must provide the office of education and vocational rehabilitation certification with each rehabilitation counselor's professional credentials. The following are qualifications required of vocational rehabilitation professionals:

1) a master's degree in vocational rehabilitation or an allied social science, such as physical therapy, occupational therapy, psychology, social work, nursing, or guidance and counseling, and a minimum of one year's work experience in vocational rehabilitation;
2) a bachelor's degree and a minimum of five years' work experience in vocational rehabilitation, unless the bachelor's degree is in vocational

rehabilitation, nursing, or an allied social science, in which case the counselor shall have attained at least two years' work experience in vocational rehabilitation; or

3) a minimum of ten years work experience in vocational rehabilitation;
4) registered nurses with three years' experience in vocational rehabilitation; or
5) licensure as a rehabilitation counselor from the board of allied mental health and human services professions.

The goal of vocational rehabilitation (VR) is to return the injured worker to work earnings as close as possible to what the earnings were prior to their injury or illness. VR services cover all non-medical services that are required to return an injured worker to a suitable job. Services may include: evaluation of capabilities, vocational testing, counseling or guidance, workplace modifications, and/or job placement assistance/formal retraining.

Access to Medical Care

An injured worker is required to select and receive their initial medical treatment from physicians who are affiliated with a Preferred Provider Arrangement (PPA).

Fee Schedule Guidelines

State fee schedule compliance is mandatory.

Medical Necessity and Medical Treatment Guidelines

Insurers and self-insurers are required to undertake utilization review for health services rendered to injured workers, either by performing utilization review or by subcontracting with a Commonwealth approved agent who conducts utilization review services. If an insurer or self-insurer chooses to perform utilization review independently, the program must be pre-approved by the state. Utilization review programs must remain separate and distinct from case management and all other claim functions. Utilization review organizations conducting Massachusetts reviews at multiple sites must seek separate approval for each site.

The state has treatment guidelines but they are not mandatory, and it is expected that up to 10 percent of treatments may deviate from the guidelines. The guidelines provide guidance to clinicians, insurers, utilization review agents and other concerning what falls into an acceptable range of treatment.

Permanent Impairment Rating

The state certified physicians use the sixth edition of the American Medical Association's (AMA) *Guides to Evaluation Permanent Impairment* when evaluating impairments when certain criteria are required to meet permanent conditions.

The Department of Industrial Accidents (DIA) has developed a roster of impartial physicians who qualify as board certified specialists contracted to the state to render impairment ratings. Certified physicians serving on the state roster are eligible to be chosen by the DIA to examine injured workers involved in pending medical-issue disputes. A formal hearing may not be conducted until a physician from this roster examines the injured worker and renders a written decision acceptable to the Department addressing:

- whether an impairment of function exists;
- whether the impairment is total or partial,
- temporary or permanent in nature;
- whether the impairment of function contributed to or caused the injury or illness arising out of employment.

A lump sum payment is a settlement or contract between the injured worker, the insurer, and in some cases the employer. A lump sum payment is a one-time payment made in place of the injured worker's weekly compensation benefits. When an injured worker accepts a settlement, the injured worker gives up certain rights to future benefits. The insurance carrier and the injured worker must agree to accept a lump sum settlement before an agreement is reached.

MICHIGAN

Health Care Services Division
Workers' Compensation Agency
Michigan Department of Labor and Economic Growth
P O Box 30016
Lansing, Michigan 48909
Telephone: (888) 396-5041 (toll free)

State Website: www.michigan.gov/wca

State Rules and Regulations for Case Management

The State Service Delivery Guidelines apply to two primary areas: Medical Case Management Services, and Vocational Rehabilitation Services. The integration of vocational services with medical case management can accelerate the return to work process, maximize outcomes and manage benefit expenditures.

Case Management Services

The state adopted the following processes for case managers to implement for case management services:
1) To coordinate all case management activities including collaborating with all medical professionals, service providers, insurers, injured workers, and for achieving optimal outcomes.
2) To facilitate all medically necessary services that include but are not limited to coordinating inpatient, outpatient, and home care services, and medical management and home modification as needed.
3) To advocate and educate injured workers in directing self-care in medical decision-making to achieve independence.
4) To develop and implement an action plan that includes time frames and functional outcome measures.

Vocational Rehabilitation Services

The goal of rehabilitation services is to coordinate timely and effective health care and facilitate the return of an injured worker to suitable productive employment. The rehabilitation process includes coordinating a multidisciplinary team in managing the care for the injured worker. Rehabilitation services are provided by many professionals with varying degrees of expertise in numerous settings.

Vocational rehabilitation professionals are required to develop an action plan to facilitate an early return-to-work that prevents an injured worker from re-injury which may occur if re-entry in the work place is not planned.

Vocation rehabilitation professions are required by the state to possess the following abilities, skills and knowledge in the following areas:

1) Assessment and evaluation of individuals with disabilities, and collaborating with medical and professional personnel to determine type and degree of disability, eligibility for service, and feasibility of vocational rehabilitation;
2) accepting or recommending acceptance of suitable candidates for service;
3) determining suitable jobs or businesses consistent with client's desires, aptitudes, and physical, mental, and emotional abilities;
4) planning and arranging for clients to study or train for jobs;
5) assisting clients with personal adjustment throughout the rehabilitation program;
6) assisting clients to obtain medical, psychological, or other services if needed; and
7) promoting and developing job openings and placing qualified applicants in employment.

The state requires at least one member of the facility's staff to have a working knowledge of the Workers' Disability Compensation Act, and meet one of the following minimum qualification criteria below:

1) Possess a Bachelor's Degree in a field related to rehabilitation counseling, have three years of full-time experience as a Vocational Rehabilitation Counselor beyond the trainee level, or equivalent experience in the evaluation, training and placement of disabled adults under the direct supervision of a qualified rehabilitation practitioner meeting the standards of this section; or
2) Possess an unrelated Master's Degree or Bachelor's Degree and have five years of full time experience as a Vocational Rehabilitation Counselor, or equivalent experience in the evaluation, training and placement of disabled adults under the direct supervision of a qualified rehabilitation practitioner.

Access to Medical Care

An injured worker is required to be treated by a medical provider selected by the employer during the first ten days post injury. After the initial first ten days of care, the injured worker is entitled to select a medical provider of his or her own choice. The injured worker can then continue medical care with the selected provider unless the employer or insurance carrier demonstrates to the Bureau of Workers' Disability Compensation that this choice is unreasonable.

The injured worker may choose another treating physician after the first ten days of care for the injury, but the injured worker must notify the employer of the name of the chosen practitioner.

State Fee Schedule Guidelines

State fee schedule compliance is mandatory.

Medical Necessity and Medical Treatment Guidelines

The State regulations require that insurance carriers must have a health care review program to provide medical utilization review services as listed below:
1) The insurance carrier is required to conduct both a technical health care review program, and a professional health care review process.
2) The health care review process must be conducted on all bills submitted by a provider for medical care services that cover on-the-job injuries or illnesses related to employment.

Permanent Impairment Rating

Payments are made for permanent total disability (PTD) based upon a percentage of the worker's wage, subject to weekly minimum and maximum payment amounts. Payments for PTD continue for the duration of the disability. Benefits may be subject to an offset for Unemployment Insurance benefits.

An injured worker who is totally and permanently disabled is entitled to benefits under the state's worker's compensation act. The state reimburses for impairments based on a wage-loss system. The state's benefit schedule limits impairment to amputations and partial amputations. The injured worker is entitled to compensation equal to 80 percent of the employee's after-tax average weekly wages, with a maximum benefit of 800 weeks from the injury date.

MINNESOTA

Minnesota Department of Labor and Industry
443 Lafayette Road N.
St. Paul, MN 55155
Telephone: (651) 284-5005 or (800) 342-5354 (toll free)
TTY: (651) 297-4198

State Website: www.doli.state.mn.us/workcomp.asp

State Rules and Regulations for Case Management
Case management for an employee covered by a managed care plan is required to be provided by a licensed or registered health care professional. Case managers are required to have at least one year's experience in workers' compensation.

Role of Case Manager
The medical case manager will monitor, evaluate, and coordinate the delivery of quality, cost-effective medical treatment, and other health services needed by an injured worker, and must promote an appropriate, prompt return to work. Medical case managers should facilitate communication between the injured worker, employer, insurer, medical provider, managed care plan, and any assigned qualified rehabilitation consultant to achieve these goals. The managed care plan will describe in its application for certification how injured workers will be selected for case management, the services to be provided, and who will provide the services.

Medical Case Management
If the injured worker is covered by a workers' compensation certified managed care plan:
1) the employer must post a notice that shows how to obtain treatment using the managed care plan and provide the name and phone number of a contact person;

2) injured workers may request of the employer, the insurer or the certified managed care plan staff for a list of providers in the plan; and

3) a medical case-manager might be assigned to coordinate the delivery of health care for your injury.

Vocational Rehabilitation Services

A rehabilitation consultation is used to determine whether an employee is a qualified injured worker for rehabilitation services. An employee must be a qualified injured worker before a rehabilitation plan is implemented.

A qualified rehabilitation consultant must possess at least one of the following credentials:
1) certified by the Commission on Rehabilitation Counselor Certification as a certified rehabilitation counselor; or
2) certified by the Certification of Disability Management Specialists Commission as a certified disability management specialist.

A qualified rehabilitation consultant, or qualified rehabilitation consultant intern registered with the department before July 1, 2005, may either continue to meet the certification requirements in effect at the time of initial registration or meet prior certification requirements.

If the injured worker, employer, or commissioner requests a rehabilitation consultation, the insurer shall arrange for a rehabilitation consultation services by a qualified rehabilitation consultant to take place within fifteen calendar days of the insurer's receipt of the request.

If the insurer requests a waiver of rehabilitation services which is denied by the Commissioner, the insurer is required to arrange for a rehabilitation consultation by a qualified rehabilitation consultant to take place within fifteen calendar days of the notification that the waiver request has not been granted.

Access to Medical Care

The injured worker must be treated by a medical provider within the certified managed care plan *unless:*
1) the injured worker requires emergency medical care;

2) the injured worker receives care from another health care provider who is able to treat their injury and has treated them at least twice in the past two years or who has a documented history of treating them; or
3) the injured worker lives or works too far from a health care provider in the plan. (There is a thirty-mile limit in the seven-county Twin Cities area and a fifty-mile limit in all other areas.)

State Fee Schedule Guidelines
The state fee schedule is mandatory.

Medical Necessity and Medical Treatment Guidelines
The Managed Care Organization is required to implement a program for utilization review. The program must include the collection, review, and analysis of group data to improve overall quality of care and efficient use of resources. In its application for certification, the managed care plan must specify the data that will be collected, how the data will be analyzed, and how the results will be applied to improve patient care and increase cost-effectiveness of treatment.

Permanent Impairment Rating
Only the impairment categories in the Minnesota schedules may be used when rating the extent of a disability. Where a category represents the disabling condition, the disability determination should not be based on the accumulation of lesser included categories. If more than one category may apply to a condition, the category most closely representing the condition shall be selected. Where more than one category is necessary to represent the disabling condition, categories should be selected to avoid double compensation for any part of a condition.

The percentages of disability to the whole body as set forth in two or more categories cannot be averaged, prorated, or otherwise deviated from, unless specifically provided in the schedule. Unless provided otherwise, where an impairment must be rated under more than one category, the ratings must be combined using a formula as provided in Minnesota statutes. With respect to the musculoskeletal schedule, the percent of whole body disability for motor or sensory loss of a member may not exceed the percent of whole body disability for amputation of that member.

MISSISSIPPI

Mississippi Workers' Compensation Commission
1428 Lakeland Drive
Jackson, MS 39216
Telephone: (866) 473-6922 (toll free)

State Website: www.mwcc.state.ms.us

State Rules and Regulations for Case Management

Case Management

Use of case management is optional in Mississippi. The state defines case management as the clinical and administrative process in which timely, individualized, and cost-effective medical rehabilitation services are implemented, coordinated, and evaluated by a nurse or other case manager employed by the payer, on an ongoing basis for employees who have sustained an injury or illness.

Vocational Rehabilitation

The Rehabilitation Department reviews all First Report of Injuries that are reported. The purpose is to identify the catastrophically injured worker. The commission cooperates with federal, state, and local agencies in the rehabilitation of handicapped workers, and promptly reports to the proper authority industrial injury cases in which retraining or job placement may be needed.

Access to Medical Care

The Workers' Compensation Law provides that an injured worker has the right to select one medical provider of his or her own choosing to render treatment. The chosen medical provider may make one referral of the worker to another specialist to continue treatment without any approval from the employer or its insurance carrier.

Any additional selections or referrals should be approved in advance by the employer or the employer's insurance carrier. The injured worker is not limited to a licensed medical physician and may choose, for example, a chiropractor for treatment.

State Fee Schedule Guidelines

Mississippi uses a Fee Schedule, including Cost Containment and Utilization Management rules and guidelines, established in order to implement a medical cost containment program. The state has a mandatory fee schedule.

Requests for dispute resolution will be reviewed and decided by the Cost Containment Division of the Commission within thirty days of receipt of the request, unless additional time is required to accommodate a requested Peer Review.

Medical Necessity and Medical Treatment Guidelines

The Mississippi Workers' Compensation Commission requires mandatory utilization review of certain medical services and charges associated with the provision of medical treatment subject to the State Fee Schedule. Utilization review is required for all services or treatment with prior authorization under the Mississippi's General Rules Schedule.

A determination by a utilization review organization or agent is required a hospital admission, extension of stay, or other health care services. The information provided must meet the clinical requirements for medical necessity, appropriateness, level of care, or effectiveness under the requirements of the workers' compensation program.

Permanent Impairment Rating

Mississippi has adopted the sixth edition of the AMA *Guide.* For an injured worker permanently and totally disabled, payments will be made for a maximum period of weeks. For injuries which result in less than permanent and total disability, the time limit for payments may vary according to the nature of the injury and disability. In cases of death, payments to dependents may not exceed 450 weeks.

MISSOURI

Missouri Division of Workers' Compensation (Central Office)
P.O. Box 58
Jefferson City, MO 65102-0058
Telephone: (573) 751-4231

State Website: www.sos.mo.gov/adrules/csr/current/8csr/8csr.asp

State Rules and Regulations for Case Management

Missouri has not established a case management state plan but does endorse use of vocational rehabilitation services as a cost containment measure.

The state mandates that a facility or institution that provides rehabilitation services, as well as rehabilitation practitioners, must be certified by the Division of Workers' Compensation. The Division adopts the certification of the facilities and hospitals that are accredited by the Joint Commission on Accreditation of Hospitals or the Joint Commission on Accreditation of Rehabilitation facilities or the American Osteopathic Association.

The Division of Workers' Compensation administers a program employers may use to provide vocational rehabilitation to severely injured workers. The employee must have sustained a workplace injury of sufficient severity. The injured worker may receive vocational rehabilitation services, if authorized by the employer that are reasonably necessary to restore the injured worker to suitable and gainful employment.

The Division has the responsibility to ensure that qualified practitioners and facilities are available and have the capability of providing the appropriate rehabilitation services for the injuries sustained. The Division also has the responsibility of reviewing the written plan of care to ensure that the injured worker is restored to suitable gainful employment.

Access to Medical Care

The employer or the insurer has the right to choose the treating medical provider. The employer can delegate that right to the insurance carrier. This does not necessarily mean that the insurance company directs the injured worker's medical care; the treating physician selected or authorized by the employer/insurer directs the medical care using his or her own independent medical judgment. Though the employer can delegate the right to select the medical care providers to the insurance carrier, it is the employers right. Therefore, if the employer and the insurance carrier disagree on the treating medical provider, the employer's decision should prevail.

If the injured worker desires a change of physician, they shall have the right to select another physician, or surgeon, but at their own expense. Therefore, the injured worker can choose his or her own medical provider, but at their own expense.

The employer/insurer has a qualified right to select or authorize a change in physician if the employer/insurer disagrees with the authorized treating physician treatment plan.

State Fee Schedule Guidelines

There is no mandatory state fee schedule in Missouri.

Medical Necessity and Medical Treatment Guidelines

State utilization review is not mandatory. In a reasonable medical fee dispute (MFD), it must be determined that the employer/insurer has authorized treatment for a recognized workers' compensation injury and has paid a portion of the bill. The issue to be determined in this type of dispute is the fairness and reasonableness of the charges for medical treatment. When this type of dispute is filed, a review will proceed separately from the underlying case. The injured worker is not a party to a reasonable medical fee dispute and his or her right to workers' compensation benefits cannot be jeopardized by the dispute. If the medical care provider and the employer/insurer are unable to reach a resolution of the dispute independently, the medical care provider must file an application with the Division to proceed.

Permanent Impairment Rating

The state requires that after a medical provider has administered all care required for an injured worker to recover and the injured worker remains physically unable, and is determined to have a disability, the medical provider can make a determination of permanent impairment. The disability will be "permanent," meaning the injured worker will suffer the effect of the injury from that point on. The disability can be total—meaning the injured worker is unable to perform any work—or "partial"—meaning the injured worker is able to work but with limitations or restrictions on what they are capable of doing. If the injured worker is determined to be permanently and totally disabled, state workers' compensation benefits will continue for the rest of their life. If the disability is a permanent partial disability (PPD), the legislature has established a formula to convert that disability into a dollar amount. The maximum weekly wage amount for a permanent partial disability is less than the maximum for the temporary total disability because the disability is partial instead of total. This compensation is for the disability only. The Workers' Compensation Law does not provide compensation for pain and suffering.

MONTANA

Montana Workers' Compensation Regulations Bureau
Beck Building
1805 Prospect Avenue
Helena, MT 59601
Telephone: (406) 444-6541

State Website: erd.dli.mt.gov/workers-comp-regulations-bureau.html

State Rules and Regulations for Case Management

Montana has not established a case management state plan but does endorse use of vocational rehabilitation services as a cost containment measure.

Vocational Rehabilitation Services

Rehabilitation services provided under the state's guidelines must be delivered through a rehabilitation counselor certified by the Commission on Rehabilitation Counselor Certification.

Prior to, or upon termination of, temporary total disability benefits to a disabled worker, a rehabilitation provider must be designated by the insurer or the division will require them to do so. If maximum healing has been reached by a disabled worker and the insurer has not designated a rehabilitation provider, the insurer will pay total rehabilitation benefits to the disabled worker and the twenty-six week period will not start until the rehabilitation provider is designated.

Access to Medical Care

The injured worker has a duty to select a treating physician. Initial treatment in an emergency room or urgent care facility is not a selection of a treating physician. The selection of a treating physician must be made as soon as practicable. An injured worker may not avoid selection of a treating physician by repeatedly seeking care in an emergency room or urgent care facility. The injured worker should select a treating physician giving consideration for the type of injury or occupational disease suffered, as well as practical considerations such as the proximity and the availability of the physician to the injured worker.

Montana allows an injured worker to choose a treating physician from a certified Managed Care Organization (MCO) or from an eligible list of service providers. If the injured worker does not select a MCO within seven days of the injury, the insurer may select a MCO for the injured worker. The MCO will designate a treating physician for the injured worker appropriate to the injury. Once an injured worker has entered into a MCO agreement and a treating physician is selected, the injured worker may not change the MCO or the treating physician without approval from the insurer.

State Fee Schedule Guidelines

The state fee schedule is mandatory. The insurer may initiate medical necessity review, bill audits, and other administrative review procedures to be conducted on a post-payment basis.

Medical Necessity and Medical Treatment Guidelines

The Montana State Guidelines establish evidence-based utilization and treatment guidelines for primary and secondary medical services for workers' compensation injuries and occupational diseases. The Guidelines include general treatment principles, which are designed to adequately and consistently address the functional improvement goals of an injured worker.

The State Guidelines are applicable to all medical services provided on or after July 1, 2011. (The State Guidelines establish a presumption of compensability for injuries and occupational diseases occurring on or after July 1, 2007. For those injuries occurring on or before June 30, 2007, treatment rendered in accordance with the guidelines constitutes reasonable primary or secondary medical treatment.)

According to Montana State Guidelines, prior authorization is not required for treatment within the Guidelines. Prior authorization may be obtained in specific cases for treatments received outside the guidelines. Disputes regarding treatment and prior authorization may be brought to the Department under the Independent

Medical Review Process. MCOs and PPOs are required to follow the State Guidelines, but these do not alter their payment agreements.

The purpose of the State Guidelines is to assist injured workers in receiving prompt and appropriate care, assist injured workers in stay-at-work or return-to-work options, assist clinicians in making decisions for specific conditions, and to help insurers make reimbursement determinations. The primary purpose of the treatment guidelines is advisory and educational; the treatment guidelines are enforceable for provider payment. The state recognizes that in medical practice there may be some deviations from the state guidelines, which are acceptable. The state guidelines are not relevant as evidence of a medical provider's legal standard of professional care.

Permanent Impairment Rating

If an injured worker is no longer temporarily totally disabled and is permanently totally disabled, as defined by state law, the injured worker is eligible for permanent total disability benefits. Permanent total disability benefits are considered payable for the duration of the injured worker's permanent total disability period. The sixth edition of the AMA *Guide* is used in determinations of permanent disability.

NEBRASKA

Nebraska Workers' Compensation Court
P.O. Box 98908
Lincoln, NE 68509
Telephone: (402) 471-6468

State Website: www.wcc.ne.gov

State Rules and Regulations for Case Management

According to state guidelines, for purposes of a managed care plan, case managers are required to have a minimum Bachelor's Degree of Education and credentials set forth in the state guidelines as follows:

1) Designation of Certified Disability Manager Specialist (CDMS); or

2) Designation of Certified Case Manager (CCM); or

3) Current licensure as a Registered Nurse (RN), or;

4) Current licensure as a Licensed Practical Nurse (LPN) and eighteen months supervised clinical experience and six months acceptable case management experience, or;

5) A baccalaureate degree (in a field other than nursing), current professional licensure or national certification in a health and human services profession, and at least twenty-four months employment experience, of which six months must be acceptable case management experience and eighteen months must be supervised clinical experience.

Vocational Rehabilitation Services

The state regulations governing eligibility and approval of vocational rehabilitation services state that services should be made available as soon as it has been medically determined that the injured worker is capable of performing suitable work based on their previous training or experience.

The state regulates the practice of Vocational Rehabilitation certification of counselors, and requires at the minimum a Bachelor's degree and the following credentials: Designation of Certified Rehabilitation Counselor (CRC) from the Certification of Rehabilitation Counselor Commission (CRCC), or; Certification as a Fellow or Diplomat by the American Board of Vocational Experts (ABVE), or; Designation of Certified Vocational Evaluator (CVE) from the Commission on the Certification of Work Adjustment and Vocational Evaluation Specialists (CCWAVES).

Access to Medical Care

The injured worker has the right to select a treating physician who has a prior treatment history with the injured worker or an immediate family member, with the approval of the employer. If the injured worker fails to choose a treating physician, the employer may select the treating physician.

After the initial choice of the treating physician is determined by the injured worker or employer, no further changes can be made without an agreement between the injured worker and the employer, or if the Nebraska Workers' Compensation Court orders the change. If the employer does not give proper notice to the injured worker regarding the right of selection, then the restrictions on changing physicians do not apply and the injured worker has the right to select any physician.

State Fee Schedule Guidelines

The state fee schedule is mandatory.

Medical Necessity and Medical Treatment Guidelines

The state does not require any mandate for utilization review. A managed care plan can implement a program for utilization review to prevent inappropriate, excessive, or unnecessary medical treatment to improve the quality of medical care and cost-effective treatment. A utilization review program should include the collection, review, and analysis of group data to improve the overall quality of care and efficient use of resources. If a utilization review program applies for certification, the managed care plan should specify the data that will be collected, how the data will be analyzed, how the results will be applied to improve medical care, and improve cost for effective care.

Permanent Impairment Rating

Medical doctors are the only treating medical providers authorized to evaluate permanent impairment. Permanent disability ratings are based solely on medical impairment ratings for disability; the final disability ratings for non-scheduled injuries are not based solely on medical impairment ratings for the body-as-a-whole. In Nebraska, *loss of earning capacity* is used to determine final disability ratings (these factors may include age, education, physical capacity, etc.). The state rules on determining permanent impairment are applied at the discretion of an administrative judge. Objective guidelines are not required for the determination of medical impairment ratings. Many Nebraska physicians rely on the AMA Guides or the American Academy of Orthopedic Surgeons Manual for permanent impairment ratings. These guides have not been formally adopted by the state court.

NEVADA

Nevada Department of Business and Industry
Division Headquarters Workers' Compensation Section
400 West King Street, Suite 400
Carson City, Nevada NV 89703
Telephone: (775) 684-7260
Fax: (775) 687-6305

State Website: dirweb.state.nv.us/WCS/wcs.htm

State Rules and Regulations for Case Management

Insurers may use a managed care organization (MCO), preferred provider organization (PPO), health maintenance organization (HMO) or the insurance carrier's internal managed care unit to administer worker's compensation services.

According to Nevada state law, a certified vocational rehabilitation counselor is defined as a person who:

1) Has a master's degree in rehabilitation counseling; or
2) Has been certified as a rehabilitation counselor or an insurance rehabilitation specialist.

Vocational Rehabilitation Services

An injured worker in the State of Nevada is eligible to receive vocational rehabilitation benefits if he or she is found to have permanent restrictions that prevent him or her from returning to the position that was held at the time of the injury and the employer cannot offer a suitable, modified permanent position of employment.

Access to Medical Care

Injured workers are required to select an authorized medical provider who is a member of the Employer Panel of Treating Physicians and Chiropractors. Insurers may use a managed care organization (MCO), preferred provider organization (PPO), health maintenance organization (HMO) or the insurance carrier's internal managed care unit.

The state describes nurse case managers as having the clinical expertise in assessing and developing treatment plans for occupational injuries. By use of nationally recognized treatment guidelines, case managers can assertively manage the injured worker's rehabilitation; by promoting modified or transitional-duty opportunities that result in cost-effective outcomes, the practice of case management activities has demonstrated a positive impact on the injured worker's total cost of risk.

State Fee Schedule Guidelines

The state fee schedule is mandatory.

Medical Necessity and Medical Treatment Guidelines

The state does not require utilization review when the state rules are applied. Nevada requires that an external review organization be issued a certificate to conduct external utilization reviews and may charge fees to conduct such external review services.

The fees are required to be:
1) reasonable;
2) may not exceed the fees set forth in the schedule of fees submitted by the external review organization to the commissioner; and
3) maintain compliance with all applicable statutes and regulations.

Permanent Impairment Rating

When an injured worker's treating physician reports to the insurer that there may be a permanent impairment, the adjuster is required to schedule an impairment evaluation with a rating physician. The impairment percentage determined by the rating physician results in a monetary settlement known as a permanent partial disability award (PPD). Rating physicians may be chiropractors and medical physicians who have taken a test on how to determine permanent impairment using the criteria in the AMA *Guides to Evaluation of Permanent Impairment* (currently the fifth edition is in use). The state maintains a rotating list of rating physicians maintained by the State of Nevada Division of Industrial Relations.

The PPD award is calculated by using the percentage of impairment given by the rating doctor, the average monthly wage of the injured worker, and the injured worker's age at the time the award is calculated. Injured workers may elect to receive up to the equivalent of a 25 percent PPD impairment in a lump sum, with the remainder of any percentage over 25 percent payable in installments until the injured worker is seventy years-old. The PPD percentage governs the length of work retraining program that can be offered to an injured worker who needs vocational retraining to return to the work force.

NEW HAMPSHIRE

New Hampshire Department of Labor
Workers' Compensation Division
NH Department of Labor
95 Pleasant Street
Concord, NH 03301
Telephone: (603) 271-3176, toll free or (800) 272-4353 (toll free)

State Website: www.nh.gov/insurance/pc/workerscomp/faq.htm

State Rules and Regulations for Case Management

The state regulates a managed care program that meets the following service requirements:

1) In-patient and out-patient case management services that include medical, vocational, and rehabilitation case management;
2) Prospective and concurrent review, discharge planning, work-conditioning and return to work programs;
3) Injury management facilitators who may manage an injured employee's medical care by interacting with the employee, treating physician;
4) Healthcare providers and the employer to facilitate the expeditious intervention of medical treatment and an early return to work.
5) Injury management facilitators employed or contracted by the managed care organization may be qualified in one or more of the following areas and have at least one year experience in the medical management of workers' compensation claims and holds:
6) State license as a registered nurse;
7) A designation as a certified case manager issued by the Commission for Case Manager Certification;
8) A designation as a certified rehabilitation counselor issued by the Commission on Rehabilitation Counselor Certification;
9) A designation as a certified disability management specialist issued by The Commission on Disability Management Specialists; or

10) Approval issued by the Commissioner of Labor and advisory Council as a Certified Vocational Rehabilitation Providers (CVRP).

Vocational Rehabilitation Services

Vocational Rehabilitation is the provision of services that are designated to restore the injured worker to, or as close as possible to, his or her prior earning capacity as measured by the employee's average weekly wage.

The state may provide Vocational Rehabilitation services in a variety of settings but, Workers' Compensation Vocational Rehabilitation is provided by private rehabilitation companies that are staffed by Certified Vocational Rehabilitation Providers. The services they provide are regulated and monitored by the Department of Labor to ensure compliance with the law.

Vocational Rehabilitation services are provided by individuals who are Certified Vocational Rehabilitation Providers (CVRP). This designation is acquired through training, experience, and/or national certification. For New Hampshire workers' compensation cases, the CVRP designation is required for those who provide Vocational Rehabilitation services. This designation certifies that the individual providing Vocational Rehabilitation services to the injured worker is qualified and is aware of the laws and ethics involved in practice.

The CVRP is required to meet at least one of the categories below:
1) current certified rehabilitation counselor (CRC)
2) current certified disability management specialist (CDMS)
3) current certified vocational evaluator (CVE).

Access to Medical Care

Within the managed care provider network; the injured worker has the right to choose a physician or other health care provider from within the provider network, and is allowed to make one change in medical provider within the network at each level of treatment. If there is no managed care program, the treating medical provider's selection is determined by the injured worker.

State Fee Schedule Guidelines

There are no state medical fee schedules.

Medical Necessity and Medical Treatment Guidelines

There is no mandatory utilization review. Insurers are required to pay 100 percent of medical cost as long as the bills are reasonable and necessary.

All medical bills that are reasonable, necessary, and causally related to the work related injury should be paid. Insurance carriers and self-insurers sometimes offer pre-approved payments of medical bills for medical treatment that are causally related to the work injury. Under the New Hampshire workers' compensation law, insurance carriers and self-insurers are not required to pre-approve payments for medical treatment, unless it has been ordered by the Department of Labor (DOL).

Permanent Impairment Rating

The state requires that all Scheduled Permanent Impairment Awards provide the requirements for assessment and payment of permanency. An assessment of permanent impairment for purposes of workers' compensation should occur at maximum medical improvement. The physician assessing permanency should use the most recent edition of the AMA *Guidelines to Assessment of Permanent Impairment*.

A permanent impairment assessment is completed after the injured worker has reached maximum medical improvement. Once the treating physician discloses the findings to the insurance carrier or self-insured, it can accept or reject the assessed permanent impairment as submitted. If the assessment is accepted, a Memo of Permanent Impairment Award should be filed with the New Hampshire Department of Labor to approve the determination. If the DOL approves the permanency, payment should be issued.

NEW JERSEY

NJ Department of Labor and Workforce Development
Division of Workers' Compensation
PO Box 381
Trenton, New Jersey 08625-0381
Telephone: (609) 292-2515
Fax: (609) 984-2515

State Website: lwd.dol.state.nj.us/labor/wc/wc_index.html

State Rules and Regulations for Case Management

The state allows for voluntary managed care participation as delivery of health care services in the workers compensation system. The state defines a case manager as an employee of the workers' compensation managed care organization who is either a licensed registered nurse or a licensed physician, designated to assume responsibility for coordination of services and continuity of care.

Vocational Rehabilitation Services

The goal of the New Jersey Division of Vocational Rehabilitation Services is to enable individuals with disabilities to achieve employment outcomes consistent with their strengths, priorities, needs, abilities, and capabilities.

The Division of Vocational Rehabilitation Services is to assist injured workers with diagnosed disabilities that are experiencing difficulties in locating or holding a job as a result of their disability. Injured workers who are disabled and unable to work, or endangering their present employment, can submit a referral for services.

Access to Medical Care

New Jersey law allows the employer to choose a physician on behalf of the injured worker. The employer is also allowed to choose the type of medical services the injured worker receives.

If the injured worker is not satisfied with the quality of care provided by their employer, they have the option of having a New Jersey licensed attorney file a Motion for Medical Treatment with the Department of Workers' Compensation (DWC).

State Fee Schedule Guidelines

There is no state mandatory fee schedule for workers' compensation.

Medical Necessity and Medical Treatment Guidelines

New Jersey approves the use of a Workers' Compensation Managed Care Organization (WCMCO) as any entity for managing the utilization of care and costs associated with claims covered by workers' compensation insurance, as approved in accordance with New Jersey's Workers' Compensation Law. Employers are permitted to select providers of medical services for injured workers. As an alternative to the traditional approach to workers' compensation coverage, employers may opt to utilize a managed care system for the delivery of quality medical care to injured workers at a reduced premium. Employers who use a WCMCO are eligible to reduce their claims cost by at least 5 percent—based on policyholder standard premium—by selecting the managed care option, if the insurer uses a Department approved MCO.

Permanent Impairment Rating

Permanent impairment determinations are made after the injured worker has reached maximum medical improvement as determined by the authorized treating physician, following medical treatment has concluded. Any party to the claim can schedule an evaluation with a qualified physician who will independently evaluate the medical records and conduct a physical examination of the injured worker. This evaluation should result in an estimated disability rating expressing loss of function in a particular body part that impacts an injured worker's ability to perform a job. New Jersey does not use a specific impairment rating criteria to use in evaluations. Impairment ratings are determined by the treating or assigned medical provider. The duration and weekly benefit wage effects the impairment rating determination.

NEW MEXICO

New Mexico Workers' Compensation Administration
2410 Centre Avenue SE
Albuquerque, NM 87125-7198
Telephone: (505) 841-6000 or
Toll free (800) 255-7965 (toll free)

State Website: www.workerscomp.state.nm.us

State Rules and Regulations for Case Management

New Mexico mandates case management services including treatment guidelines to ensure an injured worker follows a designated plan of care.

The state has established a system of case management for coordinating the health care services provided to injured workers claiming benefits under the Workers' Compensation Act or the New Mexico Occupational Disease Disablement Law.

The state defines "case management" as the ongoing coordination of health care services provided to an injured or disabled worker, including but not limited to:
- developing a treatment plan to provide appropriate health care services;
- monitoring the treatment rendered and medical progress;
- assessing whether alternate health care services are appropriate and delivered in a cost-effective manner based on acceptable medical standards;
- ensuring that the injured or disabled worker is following the prescribed health care plan; and
- formulating a plan for return to work.

Vocational Rehabilitation Services

Vocational rehabilitation services target helping the injured worker obtain or retain employment that is in line with their functional abilities. Because rehabilitation may take years, services are based on the injured worker's needs. The types of services required may differ from one medical provider to another that other clients receive.

The injured worker has to apply for vocational rehabilitation services after an appraisal of their impairment and eligibility is determined. The purpose of a vocational assessment is to gather diagnostic information sufficient to determine eligibility. The injured worker may be eligible for a trial work program placement for a limited period not to exceed six months. During this time frame, more extensive studies and assessments may be conducted to determine whether an injured worker will benefit in terms of employment outcome from established vocational rehabilitation services.

Access to Medical Care
The employer has the right to choose a doctor for the injured worker at the time of injury or to allow the injured worker to make this selection.

After sixty days, the party who did not make the initial medical provider selection may select a new health care provider. The other party must be notified of the change at least ten days before the treatment begins. If one party objects, that party must file a notice of objection with the WCA within three days of receipt of the notice to change providers.

State Fee Schedule Guidelines
The state fee schedule is mandatory.

Medical Necessity and Medical Treatment Guidelines
The state has a mandatory utilization review requirement for in-patient medical services. Injured workers are required to cooperate with the WCA or its contractor, with respect to submitting all reasonable requested information that is necessary for providing services. The WCA or its contractor is required to report any party's refusal to cooperate to the director. Any failure to provide requested information is assumed to be a refusal to cooperate with care.

Permanent Impairment Rating
Permanent Partial Disability (PPD) benefits are paid for injuries resulting in a permanent impairment or loss of use that continues beyond the date of maximum medical impairment (MMI). The Workers' Compensation Act divides permanent

partial disabilities into two categories: whole body injuries and scheduled injuries. Two different methods are used for determining benefit awards, depending on the type of injury.

When considering whole body injuries, impairments are determined by the doctor using AMA guidelines. Even if the injured worker returns to work at or above the same pre-injury wages, the disability may also be considered as impairment.

The state maintains a list of approved medical providers who are certified to make an impairment determination. Final disability ratings are not based solely on medical impairment ratings. Objective guidelines are used for the determination of medical impairment ratings. The required guidelines are the most recent edition of the AMA Guides.

NEW YORK

NYS Workers' Compensation Board
20 Park Street
Albany, NY 12207
Telephone: (518) 462-8880 or Customer Service Toll–Free Number (877) 632-4996
(518) 462-8880

State Website: www.wcb.state.ny.us

State Rules and Regulations for Case Management

The state rehabilitation program offers special services designed to: eliminate the disability, if that is possible, or to reduce or alleviate the disability to the greatest degree possible; help an injured worker to return to work when possible; or to aid the person with a residual disability to live and work at his/her maximum capability. The Board's Rehabilitation staff includes counselors, social workers, a consultant physiatrist and claims examiners to coordinate and follow-up on medical and vocational rehabilitation services. Rehabilitation is voluntary except in limited circumstances. Injured workers should contact the Rehabilitation Unit at the Board to determine if they must participate.

Access to Medical Care

The state approves preferred provider organizations and medical treatment:
1) Each preferred provider organization is required to provide at least two providers in every medical specialty area for the injured worker to choose, and at least two hospitals in the event a hospitalization are necessary. The commissioner of health may waive requirements upon a finding that the geographical area in which the preferred provider organization is located cannot meet the requirements.
2) An injured worker may seek medical treatment from outside the preferred provider organization thirty days after his or her initial visit to a preferred provider organization provider. If an injured worker seeks medical treatment

outside the preferred provider organization, the employer may require a second opinion from a provider within the preferred provider organization.

3) An injured worker may seek a second opinion with respect to medical treatment from another provider within the preferred provider organization (PPO) at any time.

The employer has the right to transfer the care of an injured employee from the attending treating physician, whether selected originally by the injured worker or by the employer, to another authorized physician (1) if the interest of the injured worker requires a transfer to another physician, or (2) if the physician has not been authorized to treat the injured worker, or (3) if the physician is not authorized to treat the particular injury or condition.

The Worker's Compensation Law prohibits interference of the insurer, carrier or self-insured employer from improperly influencing the medical opinion of any physician who has treated or examined an injured worker.

State Fee Schedule Guidelines

The state has a mandatory fee schedule.

Medical Necessity and Medical Treatment Guidelines

Medical Treatment Guidelines became the mandatory standard of care for the mid and low back, neck, shoulder, and knee for dates of service on or after December 1, 2010. There is a 30 percent increase to the Evaluation and Management services fee schedule.

Surgical procedures are consistent with the treatment guidelines. A second or subsequent repeated surgical procedure will require prior approval if repeat surgery is required, and if the Medical Treatment Guidelines do not specifically address multiple procedures.

Maximum medical improvement will not preclude the injured worker from obtaining medically necessary care. Medically necessary care to maintain the injured worker's physical ability to function at the level of maximum medical improvement and should maintain the injured worker's function following an exacerbation.

Permanent Impairment Rating

The 2012 Impairment Guidelines are the New York standards for evaluating permanent disabilities. The Guidelines address both scheduled loss of use awards and non-scheduled permanent disabilities. The 2012 Guidelines include new impairment guidelines for non-schedule permanent disabilities, but the awards are unchanged from the 1996 Guidelines. It also includes guidance for medical professionals on how to evaluate physical function and guidance on how the board determines loss of wage earning capacity. It is expected that attorneys, claims professionals, and others will utilize these new standards in an attempt to evaluate and settle claims.

NORTH CAROLINA

North Carolina Industrial Commission
Dobbs Building
430 North Salisbury Street
Raleigh, NC 27611
Telephone: (919) 807-2500
Fax: (919) 715-0282

State Website: www.ic.nc.gov

State Rules and Regulations for Case Management

The North Carolina Industrial Commission (NCIC) defines medical rehabilitation as the planning and coordination of health care services. The goal of medical rehabilitation is to assist in the restoration of injured workers as nearly as possible to the injured workers' pre-injury level of physical function. Medical case management may include, but is not limited to case assessment. It includes an interview with the injured worker; development, implementation, and coordination of an action plan with medical care providers, and with the injured worker and family; evaluation of medical treatment results; planning for community re-entry; return to work with the claim employer or a referral for further vocational rehabilitation services for re-employment.

The NCIC employs six registered nurses who are responsible for management in different geographic areas of the state. These nurses must have knowledge in the field of rehabilitation medical management for injured workers who have received traumatic injuries as well as knowing facilities or medical providers able to assist in the recovery process following an injury. The goal of this program is to provide a professional nurse in coordinating medical care to assist the injured worker in their recovery and return to work efforts.

The NCIC authorizes rehabilitation services which are mostly delivered through privately employed Medical and Vocational Rehabilitation Professionals. The (NCIC) takes a position to only provide temporary involvement in cases to assist in obtaining problematic solutions and prefer that ongoing case management continue to be provided by Rehabilitation Professionals (RP) in Private Industry.

Individuals wishing to make a referral to the NCIC Nurses services can do so by contacting the Industrial Commission, physicians, insurance representatives, attorneys, patients themselves or any individual who is interested in the medical treatment for injured workers. The service is free and is sponsored by the State of North Carolina. The state offers certification criteria for two types of rehabilitation providers for registered nurses and vocational counselors as listed below:

1) Rehabilitation Professionals (RPs) in cases subject to NCIC rules shall follow the Code of Ethics specific to their certification (i.e. CRC, CDMS, CVE, CRRN, COHN, ONC, and CCM) as well as any statutes specific to their occupation.

2) RPs who are Registered Nurses must have a North Carolina license to practice and are subject to the requirements of the North Carolina Nursing Practice Act.

3) RPs who are Licensed Professional Counselors are subject to the requirements of the North Carolina Licensed Professional Counselor's Act.

4) RPs rendering services in cases subject to these rules shall meet the following criteria, and shall upon request provide a resume of their qualifications and credentials during initial meetings with parties and health care providers.

The state requirements for Qualified Rehabilitation Professionals (QRPs) are listed below:

1. Two years of full-time work experience, or its equivalent, in workers' compensation case management. A minimum of 30 percent of the work time must reflect medical management and/or vocational rehabilitation services provided to individuals with disabilities. The work experience should be current or not greater than the past fifteen years. A minimum of one of the following credentials must meet NCIC eligibility criteria:
    - Certified Rehabilitation Counselor (CRC)
    - Certified Registered Rehabilitation Nurse (CRRN)
    - Certified Disability Management Specialist (CDMS)
    - Certified Vocational Evaluator (CVE)

- Certified Occupational Health Nurse (COHN)
- Orthopedic Nurse Certified (ONC)
- Certified Case Manager (CCM)

2. Employed within the North Carolina Department of Human Resources as a Vocational Rehabilitation Provider.
3. The commission may modify the list of credentials contained by adding or deleting appropriate credentials.

Access to Medical Care

The employer or its insurance company, subject to any Commission orders, provides and directs medical treatment.

The injured worker may petition the Commission to change physicians or approve a physician of the injured worker's selection when evidence supports a change of physician is indicated. Payment by the employer or insurance carrier is not guaranteed unless written approval to change physicians is obtained from the employer, insurance carrier, or Commission before the treatment is rendered.

State Fee Schedule Guidelines

The state fee schedule is mandatory. The Medical Fees Section is responsible for processing bills for medical services provided as a result of a Workers' Compensation claim. Medical bills are reviewed and, where necessary, adjusted in accordance with the Industrial Commission's Medical Fee Schedule.

Medical Necessity and Medical Treatment Guidelines

Utilization review is a mandatory service for all insurance companies and self-insured administrators providing benefits under the North Carolina Workers' Compensation Act.

The goal of such plans shall be to reduce costs without adversely affecting the quality of care to injured workers. Each plan shall provide for monitoring, evaluating, improving, and promoting the quality of care and quality of services provided.

Permanent Impairment Rating

Medical doctors and chiropractors are authorized to evaluate permanent impairment. Final disability ratings are based solely on medical impairment ratings. Objective guidelines are used for the determination of medical impairment ratings. Specifically, the North Carolina Industrial Commission's Rating Guide is used. Physicians only use the AMA Guides if the Industrial Commission's Rating Guide does not cover the patient's condition. A physician will assign a permanent partial impairment rating when he or she believes that the injured worker has reached maximum medical improvement. The rating is based on the percentage of disability for that particular body part.

NORTH DAKOTA

North Dakota Workforce Safety and Insurance
1600 East Century Avenue, Suite 1
Bismarck, ND 58503-0644
Telephone: (701) 328-3800; Toll free: or 800-777-5033 (toll free)

State Website: www.workforcesafety.com

State Rules and Regulations for Case Management

The Workforce Safety and Insurance (WSI) have teamed up with six of the larger medical facilities in North Dakota to have registered nurses on site to assist injured workers seeking medical attention at their facilities. Return to Work (RTW) case managers as they are referred to, will open case management services when the following criterion is met:

1) Five or more consecutive days lost from work.
2) Any work restrictions that prevent the injured worker from returning to work.
3) A request from the claims adjuster for assistance.
4) Anticipated extended medical treatment will be required.

Coordination of care and ongoing evaluations of medical treatment is the primary goal of the RTW case manager. The RTW case managers is also responsible for assisting with return to work efforts by acting as a liaison between the injured worker, employer, medical provider and WSI claims adjuster, and providing recommendations for modified duty based on medical diagnosis. Case managers do not make any decisions on claims compensability or legal matters related to the claim adjudication. In situations where facilities do not have an on-site RTW case manager, the claims adjuster, employer, or medical provider can request assistance from WSI medical case managers.

Vocational Rehabilitation Services

Vocational rehabilitation utilizes workers' functional capabilities, education, employment history, experience, and transferable skills to develop a return-to-work plan. To identify the appropriate rehabilitation option, the injured worker may be required to complete vocational or capabilities testing.

The vocational rehabilitation consultant will assist the injured worker in understanding the process, share information relating to the injured worker's medical and vocational status, and attend medical appointments as necessary to review medical status. They are available to the injured worker to answer questions, explain job goals, transferable skills, assist with job readiness skills, and explain test results of any required testing—i.e. Functional Capacity Assessment (FCA), or Test of Adult Basic Education (TABE).

The state regulation allows self-insurers and insurance carriers to contract for vocational rehabilitation services.

On-Site Return-to-Work Case Manager

These case managers act as a liaison communicating between the worker, employer, medical provider, and claims adjuster at WSI, to coordinate the injured worker's medical care and return to work needs.

Medical Case Manager

The WSI hires staff registered nurses to provide medical case management services on claims that involve potentially catastrophic or medically complex injuries to support the injured worker in the recovery process and help them return to work.

Vocational Rehabilitation

If early return to work interventions is unsuccessful, vocational rehabilitation will be assigned. Vocational rehabilitation is a service provided by an independent contracted company. Vocational rehabilitation utilizes a worker's functional abilities, education, employment history, work experience, and transferable skills to develop a return-to-work plan.

Preferred Worker Program

The Preferred Worker Program is designed to encourage the re-employment of North Dakota's workers. The program offers cost-saving incentives to North Dakota employers who hire preferred workers, while at the same time, assisting workers in obtaining gainful employment after a work-related injury.

Access to Medical Care

A Designated Medical Provider (DMP) is a medical professional or a facility selected by the employer to treat work related injuries. All employers in North Dakota have the option of selecting a DMP.

Employers may choose a single provider, a group of providers, or any combination of provider specialties (including chiropractors). While employers can choose any combination of providers as their DMP, employers should select providers with the knowledge and training to work with occupational injuries.

Any physician changes must be approved by the bureau. Changes are allowed only after the injured worker has been under the care of the attending physician for a sufficient time for a physician to complete the necessary diagnostic studies, establish an appropriate treatment regimen, and evaluate the efficacy of the therapeutic program.

State Fee Schedule Guidelines

The state fee schedule is mandatory. The WSI bill review department employees Certified Professional Coders that must follow the AMA guidelines for medical bill coding. Medical bills may be down-coded or denied if appropriate documentation is not submitted supporting the level of code billed. The WSI rule requires submission of medical documentation along with the billed charge.

Medical Necessity and Medical Treatment Guidelines

The state has a utilization review and quality assurance program to monitor and control the use of health care services. Prior authorization for services must be obtained from the organization or its managed care vendor at least twenty-four hours in advance of providing certain medical treatment, equipment, or supplies.

Emergency medical services may be provided without prior authorization, but authorization is required within twenty-four hours, or by the end of the next business day following, prior to initiation of emergency treatment. Reimbursement may be withheld, if utilization review does not confirm the medical necessity of emergency medical services.

The state approves use of the following types of medical treatment guidelines: the *Official Disability Guidelines, the American College of Occupational and Environmental Medicine's Occupational Medicine Practice Guidelines, Guide to Physical Therapy Practice, The Medical Disability Advisor, Diagnosis and Treatment for Physicians and Therapists Upper Extremity Rehabilitation, Treatment Guidelines of the American Society of Hand Therapists*, or any other treatment and disability guidelines or standards it deems appropriate to administer claims.

Permanent Impairment Rating

Permanent impairment evaluations must be performed in accordance with the American Medical Association *Guides to the Evaluation of Permanent Impairment*, fifth edition. All permanent impairment reports must include the opinion of the doctor on the cause of the impairment, and must contain an apportionment if the impairment is caused by both work-related and non-work-related injuries and conditions.

OHIO

Bureau of Workers' Compensation (BWC)
30 W. Spring Street
Columbus, OH 43215-2256
Telephone: The customer contact center is open from 7:30 a.m. to 5:30 p.m. EST.
Toll-free: 1-800- OHIOBWC (1-800-644-6292 (toll free) or
TTY: 1-800-BWC-4-TDD (1-800-292-4833
Fax: 1-877-520-OHIO (6446)

State Website: www.ohiobwc.com

State Rules and Regulations for Case Management

The state has a mandatory managed care plan that employers contract with through a medical provider network to manage their workers compensation services.

The state defines the role of vocational rehabilitation case management professionals in workers' compensation is to counsel and encourage injured workers and serve as their advocate, while providing timely, goal-oriented services. The national associations of the six credentialing organizations require adherence to ethical standards of professional behavior. These ethical codes obligate responsibility in serving clients, good behavior towards colleagues, and honesty in professional matters.

To provide and receive payment for vocational rehabilitation case management, including the services provided by an intern, the service provider must be BWC certified and enrolled.

The Bureau of Workers' Compensation (BWC) identifies the type of credentials a vocational/medical case manager must have. A nationally recognized accreditation committee must have credentialed the service provider in one of the following:

- Certified Rehabilitation Counselor (CRC);
- Certified Disability Management Specialist (CDMS);
- Certified Rehabilitation Registered Nurse (CRRN);
- Certified Vocational Evaluator (CVE);

- Certified Occupational Health Nurse (COHN); or
- Certified Case Manager (CCM).

It is the Managed Care Organization's (MCOs) responsibility to understand the skills and competencies associated with vocational rehabilitation case management focusing on return to work and ensure that the vocational case managers, program coordinators, and interns are qualified. At a minimum, vocational rehabilitation providers are required to have the following skills, which include the ability to:

- integrate vocational, educational, physical, and psychological data
- understand testing and measurement concepts
- analyze and document an injured worker's transferable skills and write transferable skills analysis reports
- conduct labor market surveys and write these reports
- conduct and write job analyses
- identify the essential functions of a job
- establish realistic vocational goals based upon the injured worker's skills, abilities, labor market, and the BWC vocational hierarchy
- evaluate at referral the injured worker's ability to participate in vocational services and assess on an ongoing basis the continued need for these services for return-to-work outcomes
- develop and write sound vocational reports
- monitor an injured worker's progress and be able to recognize when current interventions are not effective and appropriately intercede
- effectively communicate with the injured worker, employer, physician, and others
- identify appropriate job accommodations for an injured worker and develop job modifications
- understand disability management and transitional work concepts
- understand and apply the most current version of chapter four of the *MCO Policy Reference Guide*.

Access to Medical Care

Managed Care Organizations (MCOs) manage the medical services of the injured worker. This includes treatment and surgery approvals, payment of medical bills and rehabilitation referrals. Each state-funded employer has an MCO, while self-insuring employers may have their own managed care systems. If the injured worker's employer is state-funded, the MCO will work with the physician to make sure the injured worker receives appropriate medical care geared toward return to work.

An injured worker has the right to change providers. The injured worker must submit a written request to change a physician directly to the Self-Insured (SI) employer with a reason for the request. The request will include the name of the physician and the proposed treatment. The self-insured employers are required to respond to a Request for Change of Physician within seven days of receipt. If the SI employer refuses to grant the change of physician, the SI employer will submit a copy of the request to Bureau of Workers' Compensation with the reason(s) for the refusal. The Bureau Workers' Compensation will refer to the Industrial Commission (IC) for a hearing.

State Fee Schedule Guidelines

In the Health Partnership Program (HPP), medical providers must submit fee bills to the injured worker's managed care organization (MCO) either in hard-copy or electronic format. Self-insured claims are not part of HPP. Self-insured employers pay for their employees' workers' compensation benefits. When providing services in self-insured claims; medical bills should be sent directly to the self-insuring employer.

Medical Necessity and Medical Treatment Guidelines

The assessment of an injured worker's medical care is provided by the MCO. This assessment typically considers medical necessity, the appropriateness of the place of care, level of care, and the duration, frequency, or quality of services provided in relation to the allowed condition being treated.

Concurrent and retrospective reviews are two types of health care quality assurance practices. Ohio's workers' compensation system relies on three measures when evaluating medical services being provided to injured workers. These are medical necessity, medical relatedness (particularly to the conditions allowed in the claim), and cost-effectiveness. Concurrent reviews evaluate these measures while a service or services are being rendered. Retrospective reviews are done after services have been provided.

Permanent Impairment Rating

BWC requires that the fifth edition of the AMA's *Guides to the Evaluation of Permanent Impairment* be used for the basis of injured worker disability evaluations. This publication may also be referred to as the "AMA Guides" or "Guides."

Permanent Total Disability (PTD) is the injured worker's inability to perform sustained remunerative employment due to the allowed condition(s) in the claim. The purpose of PTD benefits is to compensate the injured worker for impairment of earning capacity. Compensation for PTD is payable for life. When an injured worker applies for permanent total disability, he/she must attend an IC examination and hearing to determine if he/she meets the eligibility criteria for this type of compensation.

OKLAHOMA

Oklahoma Workers' Compensation Court
1915 N. Stiles Avenue
Oklahoma City, OK 73105
Telephone: (405) 522-8600 or toll free (800) 522-8210

State Website: www.owcc.state.ok.us

State Rules and Regulations for Case Management

The state refers to a case manager as a person who is a registered nurse with a current, active unencumbered license from the Oklahoma Board of Nursing or possesses one or more of the following certifications that indicate the individual has a minimum number of years of case management experience, has passed a national competency test, and regularly obtains continuing education hours to maintain certification:

- Certified Disability Management Specialist (CDMS),
- Certified Case Manager (CCM),
- Certified Rehabilitation Registered Nurse (CRRN),
- Case Manager-Certified (CMC),
- Certified Occupational Health Nurse (COHN), or
- Certified Occupational Health Nurse Specialist (COHN-S)

The state defines case management as the ongoing coordination, by a case manager, of health care services provided to an injured or disabled worker, including, but not limited to:

1) systematically monitoring the treatment rendered and the medical progress of the injured or disabled worker,
2) ensuring that any treatment plan follows all appropriate treatment protocols, utilization controls and practice parameters,
3) assessing whether alternative health care services are appropriate and delivered in a cost-effective manner based upon acceptable medical standards, and
4) ensuring that the injured or disabled worker is following the prescribed health care plan.

In Oklahoma, case management within the workers' compensation system began approximately twenty years ago. Case management has been found to be an effective tool to coordinate medical care, communicate expeditiously to all involved parties, promote quality, control costs, and increase the satisfaction of the injured worker. When managed care entered into the Oklahoma Workers' Compensation system in 1994, "aggressive case management" was considered an important enough component to be set forth legislatively for those programs. The benefits of case management have become more apparent over the last several decades. Case managers can now be found in a wide variety of health care settings and insurance arenas.

Vocational Rehabilitation Services

An employee who has suffered an accidental injury or occupational disease covered by the Workers' Compensation Act is entitled to prompt and reasonable physical rehabilitation services. When an injured worker is unable to perform the same occupational duties they were performing prior to an injury, they are entitled to vocational rehabilitation services provided by an area vocational-technical school, a public vocational skills center, a public secondary school offering vocational-technical education courses, or a member institution of the Oklahoma State System of Higher Education, which includes re-training and job placement to restore an injured worker to gainful employment.

Access to Medical Care

The state regulation covering the application for change of physician is as follows:

1) An injured worker seeking a change of physician should file an application with the court listing current treating physician, the injured body part for which a change of physician is sought, and a list of three physicians qualified to treat the injury.
2) The respondent may choose one of the three physicians listed by the injured worker. If the parties are unable to agree upon a physician from among the physicians named by the parties, or if the respondent fails to timely file, the court may appoint a physician from the court's list of independent medical

examiners to treat the claimant's injured body part for which the change of physician is sought.

State Fee Schedule Guidelines

The state fee schedule is mandatory.

Medical Necessity and Medical Treatment Guidelines

The Physician Advisory Committee (PAC), a statutorily created advisory body to the Oklahoma Workers' Compensation Court, has been directed by Oklahoma Statute to propose, adopt, and recommend treatment guidelines and utilization controls. The PAC is composed of nine members: three appointed by the Governor, three appointed by the President Pro Tempore of the State Senate, and three appointed by the Speaker of the Oklahoma House of Representatives. The court's goal is to regulate treatment guidelines for specific work-related injuries.

Permanent Impairment Rating

Oklahoma City and Tulsa Workman's Workers' Compensation Court rules are strict regarding the submission of medical evidence, ratings and testimony of permanent partial disability. The accepted impairment rating must be made in strict accordance with the American Medical Association's Guides to the Evaluation of Permanent Impairment, or "AMA Guides." A doctor's examination of the extent of permanent impairment should be prepared in compliance with the most recent edition of the AMA Guides to the Evaluation of Permanent Impairment.

In Oklahoma, permanent partial disability awards or settlements are not made until an injured Oklahoma City or Tulsa area worker reaches a point of maximum medical improvement (MMI). The state Workers Compensation Courts have determined that maximum medical improvement means that no further material improvement can reasonably be expected based on received medical care provided to an injured worker.

OREGON

Oregon Workers' Compensation Division
2601 25th Street SE, Ste Suite 150
Salem, OR 97302-1280
Telephone: 503-378-3308

State Website: www.cbs.state.or.us/wcd

State Rules and Regulations for Case Management

The state has adopted a managed care organization (MCO) plan which allows employers to contract service to manage their workers compensation services.

Vocational Rehabilitation Services

The state regulation on Certification of Individuals includes:

Individuals determining workers' eligibility and providing vocational assistance must be certified by the state, and on the staff of a registered vocational assistance provider, insurer, or self-insured employer's network.

1) An applicant for certification will submit an application, as prescribed by the director, demonstrating the qualifications for the specific classification of certification.
2) Department certification is not required to perform work evaluations, but the work evaluator must be certified by the professional organizations.
3) The director may approve or disapprove an application for certification based on the individual's application.
    a) Certification will be granted for five years. A vocational counselor who is nationally certified will be granted an initial certification period to coincide with their national certification.
    b) Certified individuals must notify the division within thirty days of any changes in address and telephone number.
    c) Individuals whose certification is denied under this rule may appeal.

Access to Medical Care

The injured worker will be provided with a written list of Managed Care Organizations (MCO) with eligible attending physicians within the MCO's relevant geographic service area or provided with a web address for the injured worker to access the list of the MCO's eligible attending physicians.

The injured worker is allowed to change their attending physician or authorized nurse practitioner by choice two times after the initial choice. Referral by the attending physician or authorized nurse practitioner to another attending physician or authorized nurse practitioner, initiated by the worker, will count in this calculation. The limitations of the worker's right to choose physicians or authorized nurse practitioners under this section begin with the date of injury and extend through the life of the claim.

State Fee Schedule Guidelines

The state fee schedule is mandatory.

Medical Necessity and Medical Treatment Guidelines

There are no requirements for utilization review. The Physician Advisory Committee (PAC) is authorized to adopt treatment guidelines and protocols for treatment of injuries, including, but not limited to, injuries to the hand, wrist, back, knee, neck and shoulder. Compliance with treatment guidelines is mandatory and the employer or their insurer is not required to pay for treatment which is in noncompliance with the guidelines.

Permanent Impairment Rating

Objective guidelines are used for the determination of medical impairment ratings. The state has developed its own standards with input from a variety of sources, including the AMA Guides. Specifically, except as otherwise required, methods used by the examiner for making findings of impairment shall be by the methods described in the AMA Guides, 3rd Edition., Rev. 1990.

PPD benefits are not limited specifically to an aggregate maximum. In Oregon, PPD maximums are per body part, not per claim. Awards can be made for multiple scheduled body parts. PPD is paid out in the form of disability awards rather than in additional time-loss per average weekly wages.

PENNSYLVANIA

Pennsylvania Bureau of Workers' Compensation
Department of Labor and Industry
1171 So. Cameron Street, Room 324
Harrisburg, PA 17104-2501
Telephone: (717) 783-5421 or (800) 482-2383 (toll free)

State Website:

www.portal.state.pa.us/portal/server.pt/community/workers'_compensation/10386

State Rules and Regulations for Case Management

The state permits case management and vocational rehabilitation services to improve the wellbeing of injured workers.

Vocational Rehabilitation Services

The state rule on the scope of vocational rehabilitation services for individuals with disabilities indicates that vocational rehabilitation services provided under this state plan are any services described in an individualized plan for employment necessary to assist an individual with a disability in preparing for, securing, retaining, or regaining an employment outcome that is consistent with the strengths, resources, priorities, concerns, abilities, capabilities, interests, and informed choice of the individual, including:

1) an assessment for determining eligibility and vocational rehabilitation needs by qualified professionals skilled in rehabilitation technology;
2) counseling and guidance, to assist an individual in exercising informed choice consistent with the state provisions;
3) referral to secure needed services from selected agencies through state or other agreements;
4) job-related services, including job search, placement,, job retention services, which includes vocational and other educational training services;
5) additional maintenance costs while participating and receiving services under an individualized plan for employment;

6) transportation assistance for use of public transportation systems, needed by the individual to achieve an employment outcome;
7) professional interpreter services for individuals who are deaf, hard of hearing, and individuals requiring reader assistant services;
8) technical assistance and other consultation services to eligible individuals who are pursuing self-employment or telecommuting or establishing a small business operation as an employment outcome;
9) rehabilitation technology, including telecommunications, sensory, and other technological aids and devices;
10) services to a disabled individual's family to assist the individual in achieving a successful employment outcome; and
11) specific post-employment follow-up services required to assist an individual to advance their employment needs.

Access to Medical Care

The state regulation allows employers the option to establish a list of designated health care providers.

Employers have the option to establish a list of providers which meets the requirements of the state statue. An injured worker with a work-related injury or illness must seek treatment with one of the designated providers from the employer's list. The injured worker must continue to treat with the same medical provider or another designated medical provider for ninety days from the date of the first visit for the treatment.

If an employer chooses not to establish a list of designated providers, the injured worker has the right to seek medical treatment from any provider from the time of the initial visit.

State Fee Schedule Guidelines

The state fee schedule is mandatory. The department's medical cost-containment regulations have provided fee caps for medical treatment rendered under the Pennsylvania Workers' Compensation Act.

Medical Necessity and Medical Treatment Guidelines

Utilization Review (UR) process, is intended as an impartial review of the reasonableness or necessity of medical treatment rendered to, or proposed for, work-related injuries and illnesses. UR of medical treatment is conducted only by those organizations authorized as Utilization Review Organizations by the state. UR may be requested by or on behalf of the employer, insurer, or employee.

Permanent Impairment Rating

The physician who performs the Impairment Rating Evaluation (IRE) is selected by the Pennsylvania Bureau of Workers' Compensation. The physician will decide on the impairment percentage based on the guidelines developed by the American Medical Association. Physicians performing Impairment Rating Evaluations (IREs) must meet the following qualifications:

1) Be licensed in this Commonwealth and certified by an American Board of Medical Specialties-approved board or its osteopathic equivalent.
2) Be active in clinical practice at least 20 hours per week.

The insurer is responsible for scheduling the initial Impairment Rating Evaluation (IRE). Only the insurer may request that the department designate an IRE physician.

RHODE ISLAND

Rhode Island Department of Labor and Training
Division of Workers Compensation
1511 Pontiac Avenue
Building 71-1, First Floor
Cranston, RI 02920-0942
Telephone: (401) 462-8100

State Website: www.dlt.ri.gov/wc

State Rules and Regulations for Case Management

The state requires that professionals meet one of two minimum standards to practice as a Qualified Rehabilitation Counselor (QRC) or as a Qualified Rehabilitation Counselor Intern (QRCI). For a specified fee to provide services, professionals who qualify may register for two years under the state provision after meeting these standards.

Qualifications for Certification as a Qualified Rehabilitation Counselor (QRC)

To qualify to provide services as a QRC, an applicant must meet a minimum education requirement of a bachelor's degree in vocational rehabilitation, nursing or allied social science with a minimum of two years of work experience in vocational rehabilitation, or case management. To qualify as a QRCI, individuals must meet the educational requirements and supervision of a QRC over a two year period.

In order to qualify as a state QRC, an applicant must meet one of the following additional certifications:

1) Certification by the Commission on Rehabilitation Counselor Certification as a certified rehabilitation counselor (CRC).
2) Certification by the Association of Rehabilitation Nurses as a Certified Rehabilitation Nurse (CRRN) and one year of directly relevant vocational rehabilitation experience, as determined by the Director.
3) Certification by the Disability Management Specialist Commission as a Certified Disability Management Specialist (CDMS).

4) Certification by the Commission on Rehabilitation Counseling, as a Certified Case Manager (CCM).
5) Certification by the Commission on Certification of Work Adjustment and Vocational Evaluation, as a Certified Vocational Evaluator (CVE).

Access to Medical Care

An injured worker may choose their first medical care provider. Treatment at an emergency room after the accident or by a company physician does not count as the first medical care provider. The injured worker's initial provider may refer them to a specialist without prior approval from the insurer. There are no limitations established on who may become the injured worker's treating physician. The treating medical provider is required to provide the injured worker with a medical report within ten (10) days of the treatment rendered.

An injured worker who decides to changes physicians may do so by obtaining approval from the employer or insurer and/or chose from an approved list of preferred network providers. If the employer or insurer does not have an approved list of physicians, these restrictions do not apply.

State Fee Schedule Guidelines
The state fee schedule is mandatory.

Medical Necessity and Medical Treatment Guidelines

There are no state requirements for utilization review. The Medical Advisory Board (MAB) adopts and reviews protocols of treatment for work-related injuries and provides notice of impartial medical exams required at twenty-six and thirty-nine weeks of incapacity. The MAB also records complaints against and is authorized to disqualify medical care providers who violate state treatment guidelines.

Permanent Impairment Rating

The state defines functional impairment as an anatomical or functional abnormality existing after the date of maximum medical improvement as determined by a medically or scientifically demonstrable finding and based upon the sixth edition of the American Medical Association's *Guides to the Evaluation of Permanent Impairment* or comparable publications of the American Medical Association.

SOUTH CAROLINA

South Carolina Workers' Compensation Commission
1333 Main Street, Suite 500
Columbia, SC 29201
Telephone: 803-737-5700

State Website: www.wcc.sc.gov

State Rules and Regulations for Case Management

The state refers to individuals that provide case management services as Rehabilitation Professionals. Professionals providing these services are not limited to state, private, or carrier based practice, whether they practice on-site, via telephone, or in or out of state residency. Rehabilitation professionals must comply with the requirements, rules, regulations, and Code of Ethics specific to their license and certification.

Registered nurses providing rehabilitation or case management services must hold a valid South Carolina nursing license. In addition, all professionals providing rehabilitation services must possess one of the following certifications:

- Certified Rehabilitation Counselor (CRC);
- Certified Registered Rehabilitation Nurse (CRRN);
- Certified Disability Management Specialist (CDMS);
- Certified Occupational Health Nurse (COHN); or
- Certified case manager (CCM).

Access to Medical Care

Injured workers receiving state benefits must treat with a medical provider selected by the employer or insurance carrier.

Injured workers must receive pre-approval from their employer or insurance carrier to change the treating medical provider or may request a hearing and have the Commission make a determination on their case.

State Fee Schedule Guidelines

The state has a mandatory fee schedule.

An employer or insurance carrier who reviews medical claims for payment are required to apply to the Commission for approval to review and reduce medical bills. An employer who is not an approved reviewer may solicit the services of an approved bill reviewer, but may not rely on the commission for bill review services.

In cases where the billing involves unusual or complex circumstances the bill may be sent to the commission's Medical Services Division for initial review.

Medical Necessity and Medical Treatment Guidelines

The state does not require Utilization Review Accreditation Committee (URAC) accreditation. Health care organizations, insurance carriers and third party administrators are exempt from providing agency accreditation, but must comply with state standards and procedures for utilization reviews.

Permanent Impairment Rating

The state does not require that a specific impairment rating guideline is used however objective guidelines are generally used for the determination of medical impairment ratings. The majority of doctors in South Carolina rate impairment according to the AMA Guides (latest edition); although from time to time the latest edition of the AAOS Manual for Orthopedic Surgeons is also used. Because there is no legal mandate to use impairment guides, there is not 100 percent compliance with consistent usage.

SOUTH DAKOTA

Workers' Compensation
Division of Labor & Management
South Dakota Department of Labor
700 Governors Drive
Pierre, SD 57501-2291
Telephone: (605) 773.3681
Fax: (605) 773-4211

State Website: dol.sd.gov/workerscomp/default.aspx

State Rules and Regulations for Case Management

The state requires that all self-insured employers and insurance carriers contract with a managed care plan to provide case management and vocational rehabilitation services for their injured workers. The state recognizes that all on- the-job injuries may not require a case management plan and therefore the insurer may elect not to provide this service. All managed care plans must be certified by the Department of Labor to provide services. Self-insurers and insurance carriers are allowed to contract with case managers and vocational rehabilitation counselors individually from the managed care organization.

The state case management plan is defined as one that ensures injured workers will receive medical care that is prompt, efficient, and will return the injured worker as quickly as possible back into the workplace. The idea behind case management is to save money by expediting medical care by making it more efficient and more cost effective in its delivery provision.

The state regulation on case management services includes developing and monitoring the injured worker's treatment plan to ensure that the plan is being complied with. The plan must include medical and vocational activities formulated to return the injured worker to the labor market.

Access to Medical Care

Injured workers have the option to choose their initial treating medical provider. Injured workers obtaining emergency room treatment will not be counted as their choice of care. Injured workers are required to provide the treating medical provider with the contact information of the managed care plan or managed provider for medical coverage. Self-insurers or insurance carriers are also required to report an employee's injury to the managed care provider within twenty-four hours of the reported injury incident. Medical Services may be denied under workers' compensation if a change in the medical provider occurs without prior approval from the Workers' Compensation Program or without a referral from the medical provider.

A second medical opinion may be obtained by an injured worker but must be paid for at their expense. A self-insurer or insurance carrier may also exercise a second medical opinion option by selecting another medical provider of their choice at their expense if desired.

State Fee Schedule Guidelines

The state has a mandatory fee schedule.

Medical Necessity and Medical Treatment Guidelines

The state regulations on utilization review programs require that contents of the program be documented. A health carrier that requires a request for benefits under the covered employee's health plan will be subjected to utilization review.

A health carrier is required to prepare an annual summary report in the format specified of its utilization review program activities and file the report, if requested, with the director and the secretary of the Department of Health.

The state uses medical treatment guidelines that set standards for frequency and duration of care related to physical medicine, inpatient stays and return to work requirements. Medical providers are required to follow the state's Optimal Recovery Guidelines when providing care to an injured worker.

Permanent Impairment Rating

If an injury or illness results in permanent impairment, the injured worker may be entitled to permanent partial disability benefits. These benefits are computed by a formula using the impairment rating assigned by the injured worker's doctor, employer compensation rate and a set of regulations provided by state law.

If the injured worker cannot return to their previous job, they are eligible for training to get them back to suitable and gainful employment. The injured worker should file a claim with the employer and the insurer requesting education or retraining benefits.

TENNESSEE

Tennessee Department of Labor & Workforce Development
Workers' Compensation Division
220 French Landing Drive
Nashville, TN 37243-0661
Telephone: 1 (800) 332-2667 or (615) 532-4812
Fax: (615) 532-1468

State Website: www.tn.gov/labor-wfd/wcomp.html

State Rules and Regulations for Case Management

Case Managers are required to register with the state and must qualify for a registration number before they are certified to provide services. Under the state regulations, a case manager is defined as an individual who provides or supervises the provision of case management services. Telephonic case managers must also obtain a registration number from the state, regardless of where the case manager resides. Case Managers must meet one of the following designations to practice case management: a licensed physician or licensed registered nurse, who possesses one or more of the following credentials:

- A master's degree in vocational rehabilitation counseling; or
- Certification as a Certified Disability Management Specialist (CDMS); or
- Certification as a Certified Rehabilitation Registered Nurse (CRRN); or
- Certification as a Certified Occupational Health Nurse (COHN).
- Certified as a Certified Case Manager (CCM).

The state does not mandate self-insurers or insurance carriers to provide case management services but it is encouraged if the addition of services is determined to benefit the injured worker recovery. If an injured worker suffers a catastrophic injury, case managers are required to provide at least one face-to-face meeting with the injured worker within fourteen calendar days after the date of injury.

Access to Medical Care

The employer is required to provide the injured worker with a panel of physicians to make their medical provider selection from. After making their selection the injured worker must sign a document indicating their initial choice of physician.

Self-insurers and insurance carriers are not required to offer a second panel of physicians or a second opinion. If requested the self-insurer or insurance carrier may provide a second panel. An injured worker may seek a second opinion or obtain treatment with any physician at his/her own expense. Only the restrictions offered by the authorized treating physician must be followed by the employer.

State Fee Schedule Guidelines

The state has a mandatory fee schedule, and bill review is mandatory for some services. Only medical costs owed under the Tennessee Workers' Compensation Law are required to be paid according to the Rules of the Medical Fee Schedule.

Medical Necessity and Treatment Medical Guidelines

Insurance carriers and self-insurers are required to establish and maintain a system of utilization review. A self-insurer or insurance carrier may choose to provide utilization review services or may select services through a third-party administrator. Utilization review is required in every case where the medical necessity of a recommended treatment is disputed.

Permanent Impairment Rating

An injured worker is eligible to be evaluated for an impairment rating after reaching maximum medical improvement (MMI) and release from medical care. If the injured worker does not recover completely, the medical provider can assign a permanent impairment rating. The impairment rating, combined with vocational factors, may result in a permanent disability award for the injured worker.

The state has a Registry for physicians and they must agree to provide evaluations in a manner consistent with the standard of care in their community and in compliance with the MIR Program Rules and will issue an opinion presumed to be legally accurate and based upon the applicable edition of the AMA Guides to the Evaluation of Permanent Impairment or other appropriate method. The program is available only for dates of injuries on/after July 1, 2005. Any party to a disputed claim can request a MIR evaluation if these conditions have been met.

TEXAS

Texas Department of Insurance
333 Guadalupe Street
Austin, TX 78701
PO Box 149104
Austin, TX 78714
Telephone: (512) 463-6169

State Website: www.tdi.state.tx.us/wc/indexwc.html

State Rules and Regulations for Case Management

The state approves use of certified health care networks for providing workers compensation management services for injured workers. Medical case management services provided by certified case managers are an approved service according to state rules. The state rules prohibit claims adjusters from serving as case managers. The case manager is required to work with providers, injured workers, medical providers and employers to facilitate cost-effective health care and the injured worker's return to work. The state also provides regulations and a registry of private providers of vocational rehabilitation services. The case manager must be certified in one or more of the following areas:

1) case management;
2) case management administration;
3) rehabilitation case management;
4) continuity of care;
5) disability management; or
6) occupational health.

The state requires that private providers are credentialed as a Licensed Professional Counselor (LPC), Certified Case manager (CCM), Certified Rehabilitation Counselor (CRC), Certified Vocational Evaluator (CVE), or Certified Disability Management Specialist (CDMS); and that only credentialed private providers of vocational rehabilitation services will perform vocational rehabilitation services. The state registry of providers is valid for one year.

Access to Medical Care

The state has regulations regarding the selection of treating medical providers and a change of treating provider. An injured worker who lives within the service area is entitled to the employer's initial choice of a treating provider from the list provided by the network of all treating providers under contract with the network who offer services within the service area in which the injured worker lives.

An injured worker who is dissatisfied with their initial choice of treating medical provider or with an alternate treating doctor may select an alternate or subsequent treating provider.

State Fee Schedule Guidelines

The state fee schedules are utilized depending on if an in network or out of network provider is used. The state only allows the use of Texas certified health care networks or medical fee guideline reductions in the fee schedule.

Medical Necessity and Medical Treatment Guidelines

The state requires that worker's compensation health networks have a quality improvement program that ensures treatment guidelines are adhered to, such as: return-to-work guidelines and individual treatment protocols are made accessible to all network providers. This process is regulated through its utilization review network program.

The state regulation regarding general standards for utilization review and retrospective review state that the carrier's utilization review program and retrospective review program must include a process for a treating medical providers or specialist to request approval from the network for deviation from the treatment guidelines, return-to-work guidelines, and individual treatment protocols where required by the particular circumstances of an employee's injury.

Permanent Impairment Rating

Impairment rating are based on the injured worker's degree of physical impairment which is calculated by a doctor based on objective medical observation using the American Medical Association's Guides to the Evaluation of Permanent Impairment (AMA Guides).

The injured worker's income benefits (and supplemental income benefits) are based on an injured worker's degree of physical impairment as determined by the impairment rating and pre-injury weekly wages. The state requires that the fourth edition of the AMA Guides be used for the calculation of impairment ratings effective October 15, 2001.

UTAH

Utah Industrial Accidents Division
160 East 300 South, Third Floor
PO Box 146610
Salt Lake City, UT 84114-6610
Telephone: (801) 530-6800 or 800-530-5090 (toll free; in-state)
Fax: (801) 530-6804

State Website:

www.laborcommission.utah.gov/divisions/IndustrialAccidents/index.html

State Rules and Regulations for Case Management

The state regulates that self-insurers and insurance carriers may use preferred provider plans to manage their workers compensation health care services. The state allows for self-insurers and insurance carriers to enter into contracts with managed care organizations, utilization, and bill review organizations to provide their managed care services.

Access to Medical Care

The self-insured or insurance carrier has the responsibility to designate a preferred medical provider, and the injured worker must treat with that Preferred Provider Organization (PPO). If the injured worker seeks medical treatment from any other medical provider, other than the PPO, the injured worker may be responsible for payment of fees that exceed the allowable fees of the preferred provider. Self-insurers and insurance carriers are only obligated to reimburse for life threatening emergency medical conditions when a medical provider in the PPO is unavailable.

Injured workers are entitled to make one medical provider change of physician and must notify the self-insurer or insurance carrier of this change. In situations where a treating medical provider refers the injured worker to another provider, this action is not considered a change of treating medical provider.

State Fee Schedule Guidelines

The state fee schedule is mandatory. All covered medical providers are included in the PPO network. If medical care is not provided through an approved PPO network provider the injured worker may be liable for some or all charges.

Medical Necessity and Medical Treatment Guidelines

The state has mandatory utilization review standards. Utilization review includes peer review authorization to approve medical treatment that is necessary to bring about the recovery of an injured worker. Utilization review does not include a bill review of services to determine if the correct billing was used. The state utilization review system allows for an appeals process when a denial decision is contested.

Permanent Impairment Rating

The state of Utah has adopted the American Medical Association's fourth edition of the Guides, with a completely new Utah impairment rating system to be used in place of the AMA Guides. The most recent update occurred in 2001 which clarifies ratings for spinal conditions, upper-extremity peripheral neuropathies, temporal-mandibular joint dysfunction, dental loss, and painful upper and lower extremity conditions.

Upon the state's adoption of the revised impairment guides, it reports a reduction in litigations over impairment ratings disputes has reduced to less than 1 percent. Medical doctors who evaluate for impairment ratings are expected to calculate the physical loss or impairment rating based on their clinical observations and the impairment guides that are mandated.

VERMONT

Workers' Compensation & Safety Division: Department of Labor
5 Green Mountain Drive,
PO Box 488
Montpelier, VT 05601-0488
Telephone: (802) 828-2286

State Website:

http://www.labor.vermont.gov/business/workerscompensation/tabid/114/default.aspx

State Rules and Regulations for Case Management

The state allows for mandatory managed care services for initial medical case services. An injured worker may opt out of managed care services after their initial medical treatment.

The state defines Medical Case Management (MCM) as a process of planning and coordinating of medical care services which are appropriate to achieve the goal of medical rehabilitation. The goal of medical case management is to avail the injured worker of all available medical care options to ensure that the injured worker can make an informed health care choice.

The vast majority of medical case managers are registered nurses. The state requires that MCM's are licensed by the State Board of Nursing. Medical Case Managers are required to meet the state's qualification standards related to education, licensure and certification requirements before obtaining approval to provider services. MCM's may attend the injured worker's medical office visit to discuss their medical case with prior approval from the injured worker.

Vocational Rehabilitation Services

The state provides for vocational rehabilitation services, if an injured worker is unable to perform work for which they have previous training or experience. According to state regulations, the injured worker is entitled to vocational rehabilitation services—including retraining and job placement—as may be reasonably necessary to restore the injured worker to suitable employment.

Access to Medical Care

After the initial treatment, an injured worker may select another medical provider upon giving the employer a written notice of the injured worker's reasons for dissatisfaction with the medical provider. Selection of a medical provider may also include providers listed with a health maintenance organization.

State Fee Schedule Guidelines

The state fee schedule is mandatory.

Medical Necessity and Medical Treatment Guidelines

Utilization review is mandatory and all medical services must be pre-authorized. Medical necessity, per state guidelines, refers to health care services that are appropriate in terms of type, amount, frequency, level, setting, and duration to the injured worker's diagnosis or condition.

Permanent Impairment Rating

A Permanent Impairment Rating (PIR) is a medical evaluation to assess permanent loss of function. A physician rates the injured worker's medical impairment. The most current edition of the AMA Guides to the Evaluation of Permanent Impairment is used. There are strict measures used to determine impairment, and not all injuries or illnesses will result in a permanent impairment.

VIRGINIA

Virginia Workers' Compensation Commission
1000 DMV Drive
Richmond, VA 23220
Telephone: (877) 664-2566

State Website: www.vwc.state.va.us/portal/vwc-website

State Rules and Regulations for Case Management

The state does not endorse case management and states that no insurance carrier or rehabilitation provider is authorize to provide medical case management services. In addition, employers can not limit the injured worker's medical treatment options. The state does not consider medical management as monitoring treatment. There is no violation of the state statute if a treating physician grants consent to meet with a medical provider without the injured worker being present.

The Virginia Workers' Compensation Act has no provisions regarding the licensure or certification of rehabilitation counselors and offers no regulations on this service.

Access to Medical Care

The employer must furnish the injured worker with a panel of at least three physicians selected by the employer. The injured worker is required to select a treating physician from this panel. The established treating physician cannot be changed except on withdrawal of the physician on agreement from all parties or through an order from the state Worker's Compensation Commission.

State Fee Schedule Guidelines

There is no mandatory fee schedule or administrative medical review process.

Medical Necessity and Medical Treatment Guidelines

The state provides for medical treatment cost control through two mechanisms: by designating a treating physician to authorize treatments and through a commission that reviews medical costs per peer review program.

Permanent Impairment Rating

The state Impairment Ratings are not based on specific guidelines published by the AMA. Permanent partial benefits are assigned when the injured worker has reached maximum medical improvement as determined by the treating physician. The injured worker is assigned a percentage of loss, multiplied by the appropriate weeks and the average weekly hourly wages. The impairment rating award is usually paid in a lump sum. The state does not assign permanent impairment ratings to the back, but injuries to the back can result in a permanent impairment to the legs or arms.

WASHINGTON

Washington State Department of Labor & Industries
7273 Linderson Way SW
Tumwater, WA 98501-5414
Telephone: (360) 902-5800
Fax: (360) 902-5798

State Website: www.lni.wa.gov

State Rules and Regulations for Case Management

The state has not adopted case management services. The state legislature created a statewide medical provider network to provide healthcare services to treat injured workers. The network is administered by the State Labor and Industries (L & I) Department.

The medical provider network will serve injured workers from the State Fund and Self-insured Employer's fund. The state defines "State Fund" as those employers who pay premiums to Labor and Industrial Department for their workers' compensation coverage.

Vocational Rehabilitation Services

The states may authorize use of Vocational Rehabilitation Counselors (VRC) that are necessary to ensure that injured worker become re-employable. The state has established the following credentials for professionals providing vocational rehabilitation services to injured workers:

- The educational requirements include a minimum of a Bachelor's Degree with two years of full time experience as a Certified Rehabilitation Counselor (CRC) or a Certified Disability Management Specialist (CDMS).
- A Master's Degree with one year full-time industrial insurance experience and Certification and CRC or CDMS or American Board of Vocational Experts (ABVE).

Access to Medical Care

An injured worker is allowed to see a medical provider of their own choosing. Washington law also allows an injured worker to change treating physicians, allowing coverage of referrals to a specialist as requested. Injured workers have the right to a second opinion or to seek medical care from a physician of their choice.

State Fee Schedule Guidelines

The state fee schedule is mandatory. An employer may request review of billings for any medical and surgical services received by an injured worker by submitting the written request to the department. The department will investigate the billings and determine whether the worker received services authorized under the law. If medical or surgical services are determined to be unauthorized, the department may not charge the costs of such services to the employer's account.

Medical Necessity and Medical Treatment Guidelines

The state utilization review process compares requests for medical services ("utilization") to treatment guidelines to determine if they are appropriate based on the service comparison review. The Utilization Review Program applies only to claims that are adjudicated by the state fund and applies to both physicians and facilities.

Permanent Impairment Rating

Doctors who are licensed in medicine and surgery, osteopathic medicine and surgery, podiatric medicine and surgery, and dentistry may conduct impairment evaluations of the injured workers. If more than one specialist is required to evaluate the impairment rating the claim manager should be notified.

A physician may rate an impairment when the injured worker's industrial injury or disease has reached maximum medical improvement (fixed and stable), the claim manager may ask for a functional rating for the accepted condition. If the injured worker's condition is not at MMI, the injured worker's impairment should not be rated. Impairment ratings are based on the Category rating System and the fifth edition of the American Medical *Association Guides to the Evaluation of Permanent Impairment*, which are the two widely used resources used in Washington state workers' compensation evaluation.

WEST VIRGINIA

West Virginia Offices of the Insurance Commissioner
PO Box 50540
Telephone: (304) 558-5230

State Website: http://www.wvinsurance.gov/Default.aspx?tabid=73

State Rules and Regulations for Case Management

The state allows employers or carriers to meet the health care needs of injured workers through a Managed Health Care Plan (MHCP) which operates as a Workers' Compensation (WC) HMO in West Virginia. The MHCP is also allowed to enter into an agreement with employers to operate a plan that includes a network of medical providers as well as make arrangements for service payments and utilization review programs that are authorized to settle payment disputes. CompNet operates a network of medical providers and injured workers must seek care through the provider network or obtain permission from the carrier to use an out of network provider.

The state may administer a Rehabilitation Program or may contract with public or private organizations to operate these services. Professionals must meet state qualifying criteria to practice as a Rehabilitation Professional. Qualified Rehabilitation Professionals include individuals who meet the following credentials: certified case managers, certified rehabilitation counselors, certified disability management specialists, or certified rehabilitation registered nurses, and have a minimum Bachelor's degree education.

Access to Medical Care

Injured workers are covered in situations of emergency injuries to proceed to the nearest medical center. In non-emergency situations an injured worker must select a physician from CompNet provider network. If an injured worker requests a change in their treating physician, the injured worker is required to contact the insurance carrier and request a change in treating physician in writing.

Physicians are allowed some freedom in authorizing medical care for most conditions, however, some medical procedures and specialty referrals will require pre-authorization by the MHCP.

State Fee Schedule Guidelines

The state fee schedule is mandatory. The fee schedule guidelines serve as a maximum allowable payment except for care provided and approved by the Managed Health Care Plan.

Medical Necessity and Medical Treatment Guidelines

The state has a mandatory utilization and bill review processes, administrated through the insurance carrier or its managed care services. The state has established treatment guidelines, standards, protocols, and limitations designed to assist health care providers in the evaluation and treatment of injured workers. The treatment guidelines provide time frames for injury resolution, and recommend if further medical interventions may be required. The treatment guidelines are not intended to be used as rigid protocols, but all treating medical providers are expected to follow the spirit of these guidelines.

Permanent Impairment Rating

Treating physicians are encouraged to rate an injured worker's impairments. Physicians are required to follow the state's rule to use the American Medical Association's *Guides to the Evaluation of Permanent Impairment*, fourth edition. Impairment ratings in excess of 15 percent are subject to review, and the claimant will be referred to an independent medical examiner.

WISCONSIN

Department of Workforce Development: Workers' Compensation
State Governing WC Body
State Office Building,
Room 330
819 N. 6th Street
Milwaukee, WI 53203
Telephone: (414) 227-4381
Fax: (414) 227-4012

State Website: www.dwd.state.wi.us/wc/default.htm

State Rules and Regulations for Case Management

The state allows employers or carriers to contract with Preferred Provider Organization to manage their injured worker's health care services. The Division of Vocational Rehabilitation may administer managed care services or may make it available from private sector vocational rehabilitation specialist's referrals through their insurance carrier or employer. The Vocational Rehabilitation Program may offer return to work services, career planning, job placement and up to 80 weeks of job retraining.

The private sector vocational rehabilitation specialist must have at least one of the following credentials:

- Certified Rehabilitation Counselor,
- Certified Disability Manager Specialist,
- Certified Vocational Evaluator, or
- Wisconsin Professional Counselor License.

Access to Medical Care

The injured worker chooses the treating medical provider. A one-time change of medical provider is allowed. A treating medical provider referral is not considered a change. One IME is allowed. Follow up IMEs are allowed every six months as long as they are done with the same physician.

State Fee Schedule Guidelines

State Treatment Guidelines are in place; but must be supported by another medical opinion. There is no state fee for service.

Medical Necessity and Medical Treatment Guidelines

There is no state mandatory utilization review process. Prospective reviews are only based on physician review. There is no limit on medical treatment reasonably and necessarily required to cure or relieve the injury. An IME is required to terminate medical care.

Permanent Impairment Rating

The evaluation of an injured worker is a necessary part of the medical treatment, because it combines both art and science. The final rating of the injured worker's disability should be the medical opinion of the doctor.

Doctors may consult rating guide lines on relative percentage of disability and apply more than one rating formula, but in the final rating will be based on the doctor's personal knowledge, experience and weighing of all anatomical damages and clinical findings.

The state makes a distinction in what is understood as a disability in a workplace sense and impairment. In evaluating disability, The American Medical Association and the American Academy of Orthopedic Surgeons guides are used by physicians when making this determination.

WYOMING

Wyoming Workers' Safety and Compensation Division
1510 E. Pershing Blvd.
Cheyenne, WY 82002
Telephone: (307) 777-7441
Fax: (307) 777-6552

State Website: www.workerscompensation.com/wyoming.php

State Rules and Regulations for Case Management

The state has adopted policies that administer vocational rehabilitation services upon receipt of the determination of eligibility for developing and supervising an individualized rehabilitation plan for the injured worker with the goal of returning to injured worker to gainful employment.

The injured worker must elect in writing to accept vocational rehabilitation instead of any permanent partial disability award arising from the same physical injury.

Access to Medical Care

The injured worker may choose their primary healthcare provider—doctor of medicine, chiropractor or osteopath, optometrist, podiatrist, psychologist, or advanced practitioner of nursing.

The injured worker may choose a primary healthcare provider, but may not change medical providers without a referral from the primary healthcare provider or upon receiving a written final determination of approval from the Division after request has been submitted.

State Fee Schedule Guidelines

The state has a mandatory fee schedule, utilization and bill review policy. The division will pay for medical treatment if it is: Directly related to the injury or condition caused by the work activities, reasonable and necessary.

The division uses treatment guidelines to determine coverage for the specific conditions. Prioritization is depend on the frequency of the problem(s), outcomes of procedures, unexplained variation in utilization of costly resources, quality of care problems perceived by injured workers, providers, division staff, and introduction of new technology.

Medical Necessity and Medical Treatment Guidelines

The State Statutes require that medical and or hospital care shall be reviewed for appropriateness and reasonableness and will be reimbursed accordingly.

State treatment guidelines are used for some medical and surgical cases. The state may also incorporate some national medical treatment guidelines. Currently the state lists treatment guidelines for the knee, shoulder, spinal fusion, Charite Artificial Discs, and carpal tunnel syndrome as examples.

Permanent Impairment Rating

An injured worker may be entitled to receive a permanent disability award if the injury leaves her or him with any residual disability. This is not payable until the medical condition becomes permanent and stationary, which means the doctor has stated the condition has leveled off and will stay substantially the same in the future. It does not necessarily mean that the person has totally recovered from the injury. In fact, if the doctor says there has been a total recovery, there would be no permanent disability award.

An injured worker's impairment shall be rated by a licensed physician using the most recent fifth edition of the American Medical Association's guides to the evaluation of permanent impairment. The award will be paid as provided related to the number of months determined by multiplying the percentage of impairment by sixty months.

APPENDIX A: SAMPLE LETTERS
Injured Worker Introduction Letter

Dear Injured Worker

Please be advised that your claims adjuster has assigned a case manager to assist you during your recovery from your injury. As your case manager, I will be working closely with you and your physician (s) to coordinate your medical care.

My services are offered at no cost to you. Your one requirement is to maintain ongoing communication with me to assist you in coordinating your medical needs. Please keep me informed of any address or telephone changes. Workers' compensation will cover 100% of your medical and pharmacy charges, if an approved workers' compensation physician provides your care. Your insurance adjuster is responsible for all payments related to your workers' compensation benefits, including covering travel to your medical appointments.

Please do not hesitate to contact me to discuss any changes in your medical needs.

Sincerely,
Case Manager
cc: Adjuster

Medical Provider Introduction Letter

Please be advised that in conjunction with the claims adjuster, I will be providing case management services for the above listed injured worker. This is a workers' compensation claim.

Case management consists of coordinating appropriate medical care; obtaining job descriptions from the employer: obtaining written physician approval on return to work status; attending physician appointments and assisting the injured worker in returning to work, if optimal. In the event the injured worker cannot return to work; I will assist them in reaching their maximum medical potential based on the treating physician's recommendations.

Please be advised that ERISA section 733 specifically excludes workers' compensation programs and disability income plans from the requirements of HIPAA. Please be assured that the injured worker's personal health information will be treated as confidential and will only be disclosed in accordance with state and federal privacy statues.

Please do not hesitate to contact me, if you have any questions or concerns regarding this injured worker's medical case management.

Sincerely,
Case Manager
Cc: Adjuster

Employer Letter

Dear (EMPLOYER):

Please be advised that the claims adjuster has assigned a case manager to coordinate the medical services for your injured worker. I am pleased to be providing medical case management services for your company. I will keep you informed of all pertinent changes in medical condition on this employee. When it is feasible, I will ask that you assist me in case management by providing me with a copy of your injured worker's job description. The employee's job description is the best tool we have in getting a physician to release an employee to return to work and to closing the case.

I will be responsible for coordinating appropriate medical care; obtaining a job description from the employer, obtaining written physician approval on return to work status; attending physician appointments and assisting the injured worker in returning to work if optimal. In the event the injured work cannot return to work, I will assist them in reaching their maximum medical potential based on the treating physician guidelines.

I look forward to working with you to facilitate an appropriate transitional duty job and to assist you with a progressive return to work plan for your injured worker.

Please do not hesitate to contact me at (phone) and/or (email address), if you have any questions or concerns regarding your employee's medical case management.

Thank you in advance for your cooperation in this matter.

Sincerely,
Case Manager
Cc: Adjuster

Injured Worker Appointment Notification

Dear Injured Worker:

Please be advised that we have scheduled you for a neurological evaluation as ordered by your treating medical provider. Your appointment scheduling information is listed below:

Medical Provider
Address:
City, state,
ZIP
Phone number:
Appointment
Date & Time:

A 48-hour notice is required to cancel this appointment. Please notify us if you cannot keep this appointment. Please be advised that you must attend all medical related appointments to maintain your workers' compensation benefits. Please advise the claims adjuster or me, if you will require transportation to attend this appointment.

Please do not hesitate to contact me, if you have any questions regarding this appointment.

Sincerely,
Case Manager
CC: adjuster

Independent Medical Evaluation Request

Dear Medical Provider:

Please be advised that in conjunction with the claims adjuster, I am providing medical case management services for the above named injured worker. The adjuster has assigned me to address the surgical intervention as it relates to this case.

We ask that you address the following questions or you may include in a written response.

1. Has the injured worker reached maximum medical improvement? ☐ Yes ☐ No: If not, indicate an estimated time frame.
2. What is the injured worker's current diagnosis based on your medical evaluation?
3. What are your recommendations for further treatment and/or surgery?
4. Are the injured worker's current symptoms related to the stated date of the on the job injury or/a ☐ new injury or ☐ pre-existing condition?
5. Can the injured worker return to regular duty work? ☐ Yes ☐ No: If No, why not?
6. Is there a permanent impairment from this injury? ☐ Yes ☐ No If yes, please state based on AMA Impairment guidelines.

Thank you in advance for your cooperation in this matter and I look forward to working with you and your staff.

Sincerely,
Case Manager
CC: Adjuster

Injured Worker File Closure Letter

RE: File closing for case management

Please be advised that according to your physician, you have reached maximum medical improvement and will not be requiring further medical care. I am therefore closing your file for case management.

Please contact your insurance adjuster if you require future medical care.

Sincerely,
Case Manager
CC: Adjuster

Attorney Contact Letter

Please be advised that the claims adjuster has assigned me to provide your client with medical case management. My services are an adjunct to the adjuster's claims handling. I will save your client time and money by expediting the physician orders, whether for medication, surgery, testing, physical therapy or obtaining equipment or supplies as needed.

I will not provide legal advice to your client, but can assist you and your client in obtaining the most current medical information on their condition. I can conduct research on medical diagnoses, surgical procedures as well as on prescription medications to educate your client on making an informed decision with their physician. My services are cost effective because it expedites medical care and prevent delays in your client receiving medical care as ordered by their physician. Any delay in your client receiving medical care can lead to a poor outcome, which is not cost effective medical case management.

Please allow me to demonstrate how my services may assist you and your client, by keeping you informed of all medical progress and/or changes in your client's condition.

Thanking you in advance for your anticipated cooperation in this matter.

Sincerely,
Case Manager
CC: Adjuster

APPENDIX B: SERVICE CODE DESCRIPTIONS

Code	Feasibility Assessment	Time
098	Initial Medical/Voc Review	Actual
099	Initial Meet with IW/Family	

Code	Phone Calls	Time
100	Accommodations	Actual
101	Attorney	
102	Client (IW)	
103	Client's Family	
104	Counselor	
105	Economist	
106	Equipment Specialist	
107	Hospital	
108	Insurance Company/Adjuster	
109	Labor Market Survey	
110	Nursing Services	
111	Pharmacy	
112	Physical/Occupational Therapy	
113	Physician	
114	Potential Employer	
115	Present Employer	
116	Previous Employer	
117	Psychologist	
118	Rehabilitation Facility	
119	Rehabilitation Specialist	
120	Research	
121	State Agency	
122	Union	
123	Vendor	
124	Voc/Academic School	
125	Work Comp Board	
126	Other –Explain Explicitly	

Code	Visit/Conference	Time
200	Attorney	Actual
201	Client (IW)	
202	Counselor	
203	Current/Previous Employer	
204	Family	
205	Hospital	
206	Insurance Company/Adjuster	
207	Physical/Occupational Therapy	
208	Physician	
209	Potential Employer	
210	Psychologist	
211	Registered Nurse	
212	Rehabilitation Facility	
213	School (Voc/Academic)	
214	Wheelchair Specialist	
215	Work Comp Board	
216	Conf/Team Conference	
217	Prepare for Conference	
218	Other –Explain Explicitly	

Code	Correspondence	Time
300	Attorney	Actual
301	Client (IW)	
302	Current/Previous Employer	
303	Family	
304	Insurance Company	
305	Medical Facility	
306	Physical/Occupational Therapy	
307	Physician	
308	Potential Employer	
309	Psychologist	
310	Vocational Facility	
311	Work Comp Board	
312	Other –Explain Explicitly	

Code	Professional Report	Actual Time
400	Amended Voc Eval Plan	
401	Amended Rehabilitation Plan	
402	Assist OTJ Training Program	
403	Accessibility Evaluation	
404	Attend Hearing/Deposition	
405	Closure Report	
406	Coordinate IW Transportation	
407	Extended Medical Eval Plan	
409	Initial Report	
410	Job Development	
411	Medical Evaluation Plan	
413	Prepare for Hearing/Deposition	
414	Progress/Status Report	
415	Rehabilitation Plan	
417	Voc Evaluation Plan	
418	State Work Comp Form	
421	Other –Explain Explicitly	

Code	Medical Services	Actual Time
500	Assess/Analysis Medical	
501	Coordinate Voc Evaluation	
502	Coordinate Medical Eval/Treatment	
503	Coordinate Medical Equip Purchase	
504	Coordinate Medical Services	
505	Cost Analysis	
506	Counseling	
507	Discharge Planning	
508	Health Teach/Guide IW	
509	Liaison w/Rehab Facility	
510	Medical Staffing	
511	Medical Research/Analysis	
512	Monitor Medical Services	
513	Obtain Medical Records	
514	Review Psychologist Evaluation	

Code	Medical Services (cont'd)	Actual Time
515	Review Medical Documents	
516	Research Medical Facility Svc	
517	Other –Explain Explicitly	

Code	Vocational Services	Actual Time
601	Assess Work Place	
602	Computer/Job Quest	
603	Contact w/Labor Union	
604	Coordinate Home Modifications	
605	Coordinate Voc Services	
606	Correspondence-USE 300 CODES	
607	Counseling	
608	Develop Resume	
609	Develop Vocational Goals	
610	Follow-up Services, RTW	
611	Review Functional Capacity Exam	
612	Job Placement Services	
613	Labor Market Survey	
614	Life Care Plan	
615	Onsite Job Analysis	
616	Prepare Job Description	
617	Review Voc Documents	
618	Self-Employment Analysis	
619	Research Voc Facility	
620	Training/Job Seeking Skills	
621	Voc Skills/Employ Analysis	
622	Voc Test w/Score Interpret	
623	Vocational Research/Analysis	
624	Voc Counseling/Guidance	
625	Voc Evaluation (Max Chg)	
626	Other-Explain Explicitly	

Code	File Management	Actual Time
703A	Wait Time	
706	Travel & Mileage	

*Adapted from the State of Georgia Rehabilitation Supplier fee schedule. To invoice case manager service activities, refer to the Time Conversion Calculator on page 41.

APPENDIX C: CASE STUDY

Why Case Managers Do What We Do

Have you ever thought about how suddenly an individual's life can change? I was involved on a workers' compensation file that was the most challenging case in my career. This case involved a young male who was a victim of an electrocution type injury. The injured worker was working in a trench when a power line was cut by a giant crane and the power line touched his lower body.

The injured worker underwent several surgeries as life saving measures, which resulted in the removal of half his body (a hemicorporectomy). Upon arriving on the ICU Burn Unit, I was greeted by the ICU case manager, who discussed the case in full and gave me an opportunity to read the injured workers' extensive medical record. The evidence was clear that although the injured worker had survived an accidental electrocution, several surgeries, and infections, he was not out of the woods yet. His condition was listed as stable but critical. My initial responsibilities included assessing the injured workers' medical, psychological, and social needs and condensing them into a comprehensive short-and long-term treatment care plan with a goal of having him reach his maximum level of functioning. Having to establish a long-term treatment goal was quite challenging because of the injured workers' condition, and the medical survival rate for these patients is poor. Based on these factors, I realized that to make the greatest impact on this case, I would have to use assertive case-management interventions to maximize the injured workers' chance of recovering from this devastating injury.

Upon entering the injured workers' ICU room, I was met by his father, a man of small stature with eyes that cried out for answers. He could not speak English, but I knew the questions he—as a parent—must have: *Why my son? Will he live? Will he be an invalid for the remainder of his life?* I used universal language; I gestured to him and explained to the best of my ability that I was there to help his son. The father's head nod led me to believe that he understood. I knew then that all of my future hospital visits would require the services of a professional interpreter.

As the injured worker lay motionless in bed but opened his eyes once; clearly he was medically sedated to allow his body to heal from the sheer physical shock of losing so much of his body mass over a short period of time. Imagine the impact of a multisystem body trauma: there are so many deficits that your body has to learn to compensate for that loss. It is no wonder that few survive this type of horrific body trauma. But this injured worker did—and was fighting for his life.

His physicians were amazed that he was still alive, but they did not give me any false hope. His chances of survival with the nature of his injuries and future surgeries to full recovery were poor. The medical evidence for predicting survival with these types of injuries was a day-to-day decision on what treatment modalities would work. The textbook on treatment for these types of injuries, as stated by the surgeon, had not yet been written.

I visited this injured worker and attended team meetings weekly while he was in ICU, and I spoke with the ICU case manager several times a week. This was no usual ICU case. To everyone's amazement, the injured worker's medical condition was improving day by day. The injured worker survived ICU and was transferred to the inpatient rehabilitation center. He regained use of his right arm, but his left, dominant arm had to be amputated; it was disarticulated at the shoulder level. Higher-level amputations create a challenge in prosthetic replacements. In total, he spent more than a year in a hospital setting being nursed and rehabbed back to a full medical recovery. The number of major and minor surgeries he endured was countless—let's say more than thirty, including skin grafts and debridement.

During his rehabilitation care, the injured worker learned how to strengthen his right arm and make it his dominant arm. His upper body became very muscular and strong enough to be able to use the overhead trapeze bar to pull himself to a sitting position in bed.

Keep in mind, this young man now had only half of his body; his surgeries included a disarticulation at bilateral hip levels (translumbar amputation). As a result of his injuries, he was unable to turn himself from side to side, but he learned how to roll his torso. He was fitted with a thoracic bucket to support his body in a sitting position in his wheelchair. Thoracic buckets are great prosthetics, but the skin must be monitored for pressure breakdowns as well as time limits typically of only four hours while in this type of prostheses.

This injured worker surpassed all expectations and triumphed over every obstacle. Above all, he did it with such human dignity and grace, becoming an example to all professionals who worked on his multi-disciplinary team. He had the courage, wisdom and determination to see that self-pity meant defeat—and defeat would limit his achieving maximum recovery.

As professionals, we were challenged by his decision not to accept sympathy: life had much more to offer him than sympathy. We were cautioned that he could become severely depressed based on his severe body loss. I remember one group session that included his psychologist, who reported that the injured worker was not showing signs of depression, but that he should continue to be monitored and remain on an antidepressant medication. As the psychologist explained, depression can cause major setbacks in his medical treatments. I was thankful that day never arrived.

During his care on the rehabilitation unit, his psychologist found a church-affiliated hospital volunteer group that taught English to non-English speaking patients. In one year, he went from uttering a few words in English to speaking and understanding the language very well. He learned how to paint landscapes; I have two pictures that he gave me that hang in my office as a reminder that true courage can lead you to a greater place in life.

My final goal was to transition him from a rehabilitation facility into a handicapped home setting. I was faced with many challenges in my collaborations with the multidisciplinary team, which included attorneys, adjusters, several physicians, his employer, and family. I cannot stress how important it is to develop trusting professional relationships with all parties involved in your case, conveying the central message that you are a nurse advocate for the best medical care and outcome on behalf of your client.

In the journey prior to his rehabilitation discharge, many decisions were explored, such as finding a handicap home and his desire to drive again. His physicians overruled his decision to drive, even though handicapped vans can be equipped or modified to accommodate various types of disabilities. As he drew more and more landscape pictures, I explored his interest in attending a technical college for computer graphic art. He was excited and agreed to attend. What a joy it was to see him off to college. He was happy to be around young people his age, off to a new challenge in life.

He was very fortunate in that he had a father and sister who relocated to take care of him, this allowed him to remain in close proximity to his physicians and rehab professionals who worked diligently to restore hi functional abilities. His family was truly a major support system, providing him with love and excellent home care. With a good family support system, even severely injured individuals have been known to increase their life span.

During the course of four years in managing this case, I experienced so many emotions. I was taken to another level in my growth as a professional. I had never experienced such hope, courage, dignity, humility and strength demonstrated by a patient—and it came from someone so young being the teacher.

There was such a strong bond between this injured worker and his physicians that I had never before experienced in my many years of nursing. I felt "it" when I was in their presence: they were a team who fought this fight for life together, and won. I heard physician after physician tell my client's story: someone greater than us spared his life that everyone who encounters him will see love and hope in action.

Is there a greater gift for humankind than this triumphant story? He never lost hope, never became depressed or bitter. Instead, he was an inspiration and a lesson in compassion for all of the professionals who had the privilege to take this journey with him.

In sharing this fascinating case study, it is my hope that you will apply the principles of case management that I have written about in each chapter of my book to achieve the best outcome for your client. It is why case managers do what we do!

GLOSSARY
FREQUENTLY USED WORKERS' COMPENSATION TERMS

Aggravation – the worsening of a pre-existing condition by working, either by insidious symptoms from performing job activities or from a specific incident.

AMA Guides to the Evaluation of Permanent Impairment, fourth edition – the published source required to be used for impairment ratings in most states.

Americans with Disabilities Act (ADA) – Federal legislation that requires "reasonable accommodation" by employers to adjust the workplace and job activities to allow disabled workers to perform the "essential functions" of their jobs.

Assessment – For the purpose of vocational rehabilitation, assessment refers to selecting, administering, scoring, and interpreting instruments designed to assess an individual's attitudes, abilities, achievements, interests, personal characteristics, disabilities, and mental, emotional, or behavioral disorders, as well as the use of methods and techniques for understanding human behavior in relation to coping with, adapting to, or changing life situations.

Causation – this is the relationship between incident(s) at work and subsequent injury and/or disability; for example, conditions caused or aggravated by employment are compensable.

Confidentiality of Medical Information – In a workers' compensation case, medical care is neither confidential nor subject to the Health Insurance Portability and Accountable Act of 1996 (HIPPA).

Disability – The gap between what an individual can physically do and what a specific job requires is considered an injured worker's disability. Physicians generally do not have expertise for determining disability, but they do have expertise for determining impairment.

Employer – A legal entity that controls and directs a servant or worker under an express or implied contract of employment and pays (or is obligated to pay) him or her salary or wages in compensation.

Exclusive Remedy – this is the concept that the employer may not be sued by an injured worker outside the workers' compensation system.

Fee Schedule – In many states, the fee schedule is used to determine fees paid to medical providers and facilities. Fees are determined by Workers' Compensation Boards.

Functional Capacity Evaluation (FCE) – an evaluation comparing specific physical capabilities in relationship to the demands of a job. Functional Capacity Evaluation is defined as the objective determination of the claimant's ability to participate in activities within a work setting. The FCE is used to match physical capabilities to job requirements and should address such activities as bending, lifting, pushing, pulling, balancing, reaching, climbing, stooping, standing, sitting, eye-hand-foot coordination, manual finger dexterity, and physical endurance. The FCE must be performed by a registered physical or occupational therapist or other qualified medical provider.

ICD-9 – These International Classification of Diseases (ICD-9) codes comprise BWC's top 30 ICD-9s as identified in the Diagnosis Determination Guidelines. This information will aid the medical-only claims service specialist (CSS) in making accurate, timely initial claim determinations as well as in investigating the claim for potential subrogation.

Identifying Information – This refers to the employee's name, current mailing address, social security number, date of injury, date of birth, employee's phone number, education level, average weekly wage, vocational rehabilitation referral date, Department of Labor and Industry's file number, insurer's name, insurer's current mailing address, claims adjuster's name, phone number, insurer's file number, employer's name and phone number, vocational rehabilitation counselor's name, counselor's current address, and the counselor's registration number.

Impairment – any anatomic or physiologic loss of function, measurable by AMA guidelines.

Independent Medical Examination (IME) – The IME is a medical evaluation of an injured worker to determine diagnosis, prognosis, necessary treatment, impairment, and work status. An IME does not create a physician-patient relationship. The fee for an IME determined ahead of time by agreement between parties.

Injury – an injury is any harmful, work-related change in or to the body, whether occurring instantaneously or gradually, and includes a claimed or apparent injury or disease. The term also is inclusive of damage to and the cost of replacement of prosthetic devices, hearing aids, and eyeglasses when the damage or need for replacement arises out of and during the course of employment

Insurer – an insurer is a workers' compensation insurance carrier, including the State Workmen's Insurance Fund, an employer who is authorized by the department to self-insure its workers' compensation liability, or a group of employers authorized by the department to act as a self-insurance fund.

Life-Threatening Injury – A life-threatening injury is defined as an "injury involving a substantial risk of death; loss or substantial impairment of the function of a bodily member, organ, or mental faculty that is likely to be permanent; or an obvious disfigurement that is likely to be permanent." United States v. Taylor, 2009 U.S. App. LEXIS 16394 (fourth Cir. N.C. July 24, 2009)

Maximum Medical Improvement (MMI) – MMI is the point at which no significant further improvement for any specific condition is expected.

Mediation – this process is an alternative dispute resolution mechanism available in some states to resolve disputed issues outside of court.

Medical Case Management – this refers to the planning and coordination of healthcare services appropriate to achieve the goal of medical rehabilitation. Medical case management may include but is not limited to case assessment, including a personal interview with the injured employee and the assistance in developing, implementing, and coordinating a medical care plan with healthcare providers, as well as the employee and his or her family and evaluation of treatment results. Medical case management is not the provision of medical care. The goal of medical case management should be to avail the disabled individual of all available treatment options to ensure that the client can make an informed choice.

Medical Necessity – a medical necessity refers to medical treatment and services reasonably required to affect a cure, give relief, or restore the employee to suitable employment.

Medicare Carrier – A Medicare carrier is an organization with a contractual relationship with the Center for Medicare & Medicaid Services (CMS) to process Medicare claims.

Medicare Intermediary – A Medicare intermediary is an organization with a contractual relationship with CMS to process Medicare Part A or Part B claims.

Medicare Part A – this refers to Medicare hospital insurance benefits that pay providers for facility-based care, such as care provided in inpatient general and tertiary hospitals, specialty hospitals, home health agencies, and skilled nursing facilities.

Medicare Part B – this refers to Medicare supplementary medical insurance which pays providers for physician services, outpatient hospital services, durable medical equipment, physical therapy, and other services.

Notice of Program Reimbursement (NPR) – the letter of notification from the Medicare intermediary to the provider regarding the final settlement of the Medicare cost report is the NPR.

Palliative Care – Medical services rendered to reduce or lessen the intensity of an otherwise stable medical condition. This does not include those medical services rendered to diagnose, heal, or permanently alleviate or eliminate a medical condition.

Panel of Physicians – Some states establish a panel of physicians, and employers are obligated to post whereby an injured party can obtain medical treatment for work-related injuries. If the employee seeks treatment from a physician not included on the panel, he or she will be responsible for payment.

Permanent Partial Disability (PPD) – Permanent partial disability refers to the extent to which a worker's capacity to perform work has been permanently reduced. The only consideration in paying PPD is taking the schedule from the statute and applying the physician's impairment rating. This payment is not tied to ability to work.

Permanent Total Disability (PTD) – When a worker has been rendered completely and permanently incapable of engaging in any type of substantial employment he or she may be qualified for permanent total disability status.

Permanent Partial Impairment (PPI) – See Impairment. PPI status is determined by a physician at MMI using the AMA guidelines.

Possible – when the likelihood of an outcome is less than 50 percent.

Probable – when the likelihood of an outcome is more than 50 percent.

Self-insured – Employers who act as their own insurer are considered self-insured.

Settlement – this is a legal term indicating resolution of issues involved in a dispute.

Statute of Limitations – the right to compensation is barred unless a claim is filed with the state of adjudication, usually within a year after the injury or death of the worker.

Subjective Finding – a physical finding which can be under the control of the examinee.

Subsequent Injury Trust Fund – this refers to and agency designed to reduce the impact of singularly large workers' compensation claims in the event that a worker with a disability is injured on the job and aggravates a pre-existing impairment.

Recurrence – this is the return of symptoms following a temporary remission.

Regular Full-Time Employment – this refers to a job that at the time of hire was or is currently expected to continue indefinitely with no projected end date.

Temporary Partial Disability (TPD) – TPD exists when a worker has been rendered for a period of time partially incapable of engaging in substantial employment or earns less than before the injury was sustained.

Temporary Total Disability (TTD) – TTD exists when a worker has been rendered for a period of time completely incapable of engaging in substantial employment.

Unbundling – the practice of separate billing for multiple service items or procedures instead of grouping the services into one charge item is called unbundling.

Urgent Care – Is the delivery of ambulatory care in a facility dedicated to the delivery of medical care outside of a hospital emergency department, usually on an unscheduled, walk-in basis.

Usual and Customary Charge – This refers to the rate most often charged by providers of similar training, experience, and licensure for a specific treatment, accommodation, product, or service in the geographic area where the treatment, accommodation, product, or service is provided.

Utilization Review – the determination if medical necessity for medical and/or surgical in-hospital, outpatient, and alternative setting treatments are appropriate. It includes pre-certification for elective treatments. Concurrent review and retrospective review are required for emergency cases.

Utilization Review Organization (URO) – an organization authorized by the state for the purpose of determining the reasonableness or necessity of medical treatment administered to workers with work-related injuries.

Workers' Compensation Act – According to *Black's Law Dictionary*, Workers' Compensation Acts are statues enacted to define the employer's liability for injuries (by accident) or sickness (occupational disease) arising out of and in the course of the employment relationship or responsibilities. No employer negligence is required to recover under the statues. Workers' compensation is an exclusive remedy. The injured worker cannot file a negligence or personal injury action against the employer.

US Department of Labor, Dictionary of Occupational Titles

Sedentary Work – Exerting up to ten pounds of force occasionally and/or a negligible amount of force frequently to lift, carry, push, pull, or otherwise move objects, including the human body.

Light Work – Exerting up to twenty pounds of force occasionally, and/or up to ten pounds force frequently, and/or a negligible amount of force constantly to move objects.

Medium Work – Exerting twenty to fifty pounds of force occasionally, and/or ten to twenty-five pounds of force frequently, and/or greater than negligible up to ten pounds of force constantly to move objects.

Heavy Work – Exerting fifty to 100 pounds of force occasionally, and/or twenty-five to fifty pounds of force frequently, and/or ten pounds of force constantly to move objects.

Very Heavy Work – exerting in excess of 100 pounds of force occasionally and/or in excess of twenty pounds of force constantly to move objects.

INDUSTRY-STANDARD
WORKERS' COMPENSATION ABBREVIATIONS

ADJ	CLAIM ADJUSTER
ADV	ADVICE
A/M	ACCOUNT MANAGER
A/P	ATTENDING PHYSICIAN, DOCTOR
APPT	APPOINTMENT
ASAP	AS SOON AS POSSIBLE
ATTY	ATTORNEY
2x DY	TWO TIMES A DAY
2x wk	TWO TIMES A WEEK
C1-7	CERVICAL VERTEBRAE
CM	CASE MANAGER
COMP TERM	COMP TERMINATED
C/O	COMPLAINT
CONCL	CONCILIATION
CONF	CONFERENCE
CONT	CONTINUED
CR	CASUAL RELATIONSHIP
CT	CAT SCAN
CTS	CARPAL TUNNEL SYNDROME
DEP	DEPENDENTS
DICT	DICTATION
DOB	DATE OF BIRTH
DOH	DATE OF HIRE
DOS	DATE OF SERVICE
DR	DOCTOR
DY	DAY
EE	EMPLOYEE
EHS	EMPLOYEE HEALTH SERVICE
E/P	EXAMINING PHYSICIAN

ER	EMERGENCY ROOM
FCE	FUNCTIONAL CAPACITY EVALUATION
FD	FULL DUTY
FH	FULL HOURS
F/U	FOLLOW UP
FX	FRACTURE
H&P	HISTORY AND PHYSICAL
HNP	HERNIATED NUCLEUS PULPOSUS
HR	HUMAN RESOURCES
HRS	HOURS
HX	HISTORY
IME	INDEPENDENT MEDICAL EVALUATION
INPT	IN HOSPITAL (INPATIENT ADMIT)
L1-5	LUMBAR DISC
LB	LOW BACK
LBS	LUMBOSACRAL SPRAIN/STRAIN
LE	LOWER EXTREMITY
LT	LEFT
LOC	LOSS OF CONSCIOUSNESS
LOF	LOSS OF FUNCTION
LOS	LENGTH OF STAY (IN HOSPITAL)
LOV	LAST OFFICE VISIT
L/S	LUMP SUM
MD	MODIFIED DUTY
MH	MODIFIED HOURS
MI	MYOCARDIAL INFARCTION (HEART ATTACK)
MMI	MAXIMUM MEDICAL IMPROVEMENT
MTH	MONTH(S)
NA	NOT APPLICABLE
NOC	NIGHT
NOV	NEXT OFFICE VISIT
NP	NURSE PRACTITIONER

NSAID	NONSTEROIDAL ANTI-INFLAMMATORY DRUGS
NSG	NURSING
OHN	OCCUPATIONAL HEALTH NURSE
OHS	OCCUPATIONAL HEALTH SERVICE
OOW	OUT OF WORK
OT	OCCUPATIONAL THERAPY
O.T.	OVERTIME
OTC	OVER THE COUNTER
PA	PHYSICIAN ASSISTANT
PCE	PHYSICAL CAPACITY EVALUATION
PCP	PRIMARY CARE PROVIDER
P/I	PRIVATE INVESTIGATOR
PRN	AS NEEDED
PT OR P.T.	PATIENT OR PHYSICAL THERAPY
QA	QUALITY ASSURANCE
QD	DAILY/ONCE PER DAY
4 x D	FOUR TIMES PER DAY
REC	RECOMMENDED
RCVD	RECEIVED
R/I	RECORDED INTERVIEW
R/O	RULE OUT
ROM	RANGE OF MOTION
ROI	REPORT OF INJURY
RSD	REFLEX SYMPATHETIC DYSTROPHY
RT	RIGHT
RTW	RETURN TO WORK
RX	PRESCRIBED TREATMENT
S1-5	SACRAL DISC
SG	SURGERY/SURGICAL
SOC	SECOND OPINION
S/W	SPOKE WITH
SX	SYMPTOMS
T1-12	THORACIC DISC

TCF	TELEPHONE CALL FROM
TCT	TELEPHONE CALL TO
T/D	TARGET DATE
3 x D	THREE TIMES PER DAY
TOS	THORACIC OUTLET SYNDROME
TPD	TEMP/PARTIAL DISABILITY
TTD	TEMP/TOTAL DISABILITY
TX	TREATMENT
UE	UPPER EXTREMITY
UR	UTILIZATION REVIEW
V/M	VOICE MAIL
W/	WITH
WC	WORKERS' COMPENSATION
WK	WEEK
WNL	WITHIN NORMAL LIMITS
W/O	WITHOUT
W/S	WAGE STATEMENT
@	AT
Y/O	YEARS OLD
<	LESS THAN
>	GREATER THAN
X	TIMES (E.G., 3x PER WEEK)
#	POUNDS

**Abbreviation list adapted from ManagedComp Worker's Compensation list of abbreviations

REFERENCES

"Quality First: Better Health Care for All Americans." President's Advisory Commission on Consumer Protection and Quality in the Health Care Industry. 1998.

"Return to Work." *Managed Comp, Case Management Policies & Procedures Manual.* Atlanta: ManagedComp, Inc., 1993-94. Company dissolved 2002.

2001 Report to Congress on Telemedicine; May 16, 2002. Office for the advancement of Telehealth.

2009 Analysis of Workers' Compensation Laws. U.S. Chamber of Commerce. www.uschamber.com.

Alexander, Mary Ann, PhD, RN, Nursing Regulation Chief Officer. "Nursing Licensure Compact." Chicago: National Council of State Boards of Nursing, 2011. http://www.ncsbn.org.

AMA Reference Guide to Impairment Ratings by State. www.impairment.com/Use_of_AMA_Guides.htm.

Anderson, Jane M. *State-By-State Laws and Regulations on Workers' Compensation Managed Care.* Gaithersburg: Aspen Publication, 1999.

Bowling, Maddy. "Running Workers' Compensation Utilization Reviews." *Risk & Insurance.* April 15, 2008.

Case Management Society of America. *Standards of Practice for Case Management*, Standards of Care. Little Rock, Arkansas: Case Management Society of America, (pp. 13-16) 2002. www.CMSA.org.

CMSA 2004–2005 Survey of State Boards of Nursing, www.cmsa.org.

Commission for Case Manager Certification, Case Management Practice, Philosophy of Case Management. *Essential Activities of Case Management,* Role & Function Study, 2004. http://www.ccmcertification.org.

Commission for Case Manager Certification. *Definition of Case Management and Essential Activities of Case Managers*. 2011. http://www.ccmcertification.org/search/node/definition%20of%20case%20management.

Commons, Darlene. "The Value of Medical Recovery Guidelines in Workers Compensation Case Management." *Professional Case Management.* 16. no.5 (2011): 269-271. www.professionalcasemanagementjournal.com.

Consonery-Fairnot, Dorothy, MSHA, RN, CCM, CLNC. "Enhancing the Team Approach to Care with Professional Case Management." *Professional Case Management*. 17. no. 1 (2011): 29-30. www.professionalcasemanagementjournal.com.

Consonery-Fairnot, Dorothy, MSHA, RN, CCM, CLNC. "Handling Workers' Compensation Injuries with Pre-Existing Conditions." *Professional Case Management*. 15. no. 2 (2010): 109-111. www.professionalcasemanagementjournal.com.

Consonery-Fairnot, Dorothy, MSHA, RN, CCM, CLNC. "Patient-Centered Care: The New Definition of Case Management." *Dorland Health*. August 2011. http://www.dorlandhealth.com/print/case.management/cip_magazine.

Consonery-Fairnot, Dorothy, MSHA, RN, CCM, CLNC. "Rise in Chronic Conditions Indicates Greater Need for Case Management." *Professional Case Management*. 16. no. 3 (2011): 105-106. www.professionalcasemanagementjournal.com.

Consonery-Fairnot, Dorothy, MSHA, RN, CCM, CLNC. "Why We Do What We Do: Case Managers Unite Multidisciplinary Team Around Injured Patient." *Professional Case Management*. 17 no. 1 (2012): 37-38.

Dell, C. Felix, PT and Sarah Marchant, MPT. "Functional Assessment Rehab." Salt Lake City, Utah: Strong & Hanni Insurance Law Newsletter. 3 no. 3 (2009).

DiBenedetto, Deborah. "Interstate Practice in the Age of Informatics and E-Technology." *AAOHN Journal*. 51. no. 9 (2003): 367-369.

Edwards, Adrian, and Elwyn Glyn. *Shared Decision-Making in Health Care: Achieving Evidence-Based Patient Choice*. London: Oxford University Press, 2009.

Institutes of Medicine. Crossing the Quality Chasm: A New Health System for the 21st century. Washington, DC: National Academies Press, 2001.

Leonard, Benjamin, Esq. Bovis, Kyle & Burch, LLC. *"Fraud in Catastrophic and Other Claims."* Atlanta: Educational Seminar, 2012. www.boviskyle.com.

Managed Comp Definitions of Workers' Compensation Terminology. Atlanta: ManagedComp, Inc., 1993-94.

New York State Workers Compensation Board. "Glossary of Workers' Compensation Terms." www.wcb.ny.gov/content/main/theboard/glossary.jsp.

Rubin, Stanford and Richard T. Roessler. *Foundations of the Vocational Rehabilitation Process*. 6th edition. 2007. Portland: Book News, 2007.

Service Code Description & Fee Schedule was adopted from State of Georgia Rehab supplier fee schedule. http://sbwc.georgia.gov/portal/site/SBWC/

Sminkey, P. "CCMC News and Views: Clarity and Consistency in Care Delivery through Case Management." *Professional Case Management*. 16. no. 6 (2011): 279-280. ww.ccmcertification.org.

Smith, C. M. and Maurer, F.A. *Community Health Nursing: Theory and Practice*. 3rd Edition. W.B. Saunders Company. 2004.

State of Georgia Catastrophic Rehab Supplier Standards for case management. Procedure Manual. Atlanta, 2007. http://sbwc.georgia.gov/portal/site/SBWC/

Tahan, H. and Campagna, V. "Case Management Roles and Functions Across Various Settings and Professional Disciplines." *Professional Case Management*. 15. no. 5 (2010): 245-277.

Watson, Annette, MBA, RN-BC, CCM. "Medical Loss Ratio." *Professional Case Management*. 15. no. 6 (2010): 303-304.

Weed, Roger O. *Life Care Planning and Case Management Handbook*. 2nd Edition. Boca Raton, Florida: CRC Press, LLC, 2004.

Whelan, Patricia. *Official Disability Guidelines*. (1995) Encinitas, CA: Work Loss Data Institute. http://www.odg-twc.com/states.htm.

Additional Resources

AAOHN   **American Association of Occupational Health Nurses**

    Focus: Occupational Health Nursing

    Provider: American Association of Occupational Health Nurses

    Website: https://www.aaohn.org/

ABDA   **American Board of Disability Analyst**

    Focus: Rehab, Medicine, Case Management

    Provider: American Board of Disability Analysts

    Website: http://www.americandisability.org/certifications.html

ACM   **Accredited Case Manager**

    Focus: A Certification for Hospital / Health System Case Management Professionals

    Provider: American Case Management Association (ACMA)

    Website: http://www.acmaweb.org/section.asp?sID=16

CASWCM
CSWCM   **Certified Social Work Case Manager**

    Focus: MSW Social Workers
                  BSW Social Workers

    Provider: National Association of Social Workers (NASW)

    Website: http://www.socialworkers.org

CCM   **Certified Case Manager**

    Focus: Multiple Practice Setting Case Managers

Provider: Commission for Case Management Certification

Website: http://www.ccmcertification.org

CCP   **Chronic Care Professionals**

Focus: Health coaching and chronic care certification program; focus is on all members of the health care team

Provider: Health Sciences Institute

Website: http://www.healthsciences.org/information-about-ccp-certification.html

CDMS   **Certified Disability Management Specialist**

Focus: Disability Managers
Insurance Based
Rehab Specialists
Vocational Counselors

Provider: Certified Disability Management Specialist Commission

Website: http://www.cdms.org

COHN/CM   **Certified Occupational Health Nurse-Case Manager**

COHN-S/CM

Focus: Occupational Health Case Management

Provider: American Board of Occupational Health Nursing – Case Manager

Website: http://www.abohn.org

CRC   **Certified Rehabilitation Counselor**

Focus: Rehab Counselors

Provider: Commission on Rehabilitation Counselor Certification (CRCC)

Website: http://www.crccertification.com

CRRN   **Certified Rehabilitation Registered Nurse Certified**
CRRN-A   **Rehabilitation Nurse-Advanced**

    Focus: Rehab Nurses

    Provider: Rehabilitation Nursing Certification Board

    Website: http://www.rehabnurse.org

RN-BC   **Registered Nurse Case Manager**

    Focus: Nurse Case Manager

    Provider: American Nurses Credentialing Center (ANCC)

    Website: http://www.nursingworld.org

RN-C   **Certified Nurse Case Manager**

    Focus: Nurse Case Manager

    Provider: American Nurses Credentialing Center (ANCC)

    Website: http://www.nursingworld.org

ABOUT THE AUTHOR

Dorothy Consonery-Fairnot, MSHA, BS, ADN, RN, CCM, CLNC, is the principal consultant and president of Fairnot & Associates Health Care Consulting, LLC. She has worked with large and multisystem health care organizations representing medical, managed care, insurance, and third-party administrators. An experienced nurse consultant, she serves as regional operations manager in workers' compensation case management and is a legal nurse consultant practicing in defense personal liability medical case review. She also served as Board Chair for the Commission for Case Manager Certification (CCMC) 2011-2012 and a board member since 2005. She holds a degree in nursing from Nicholls State University and a master's degree in Health Care Services Administration from the University of St. Francis. She has been a frequent contributor to professional journals and her articles have been published by *Lippincott's Case Management, Professional Case Management, CARING, The Health Care Executive, Case & Point, The Rehab Pro, Care Management* and other publications. Her essay, "When the Patient Becomes the Teacher: A Lesson in Hope," was included in the anthology, *Meditations on Hope: Nurses' Stories about Motivation and Inspiration*, released by Kaplan Publishing in October 2008.

For more information, please visit www.fairnotandassociates.com.